PSALMS

SONGS
FOR
THE WAY HOME

Paul Glynn sm

PSALMS

SONGS FOR THE WAY HOME

Paul Glynn

E J DWYER

First published in Australia and New Zealand in 1996
First published in the U.S.A., Canada, Ireland,
the United Kingdom and Europe in 1997
by
E. J. Dwyer (Australia) Pty Ltd
Unit 13, Perry Park
33 Maddox Street
Alexandria N.S.W. 2015
Australia
Phone: (02) 9550 2355
Fax: (02) 9519 3218

National Library of Australia
Cataloguing-in-Publication data

Glynn, Paul, 1928– .
    Psalms: songs for the way home.

    ISBN 0 85574 366 2.

    1. Devotional exercises. 2. Meditations. 3. Prayers.
    I. Title.

242

Cover design by Mango Design Group
Text design by NB Design
Edited by Kevin Mark
Typeset in Goudy 11½/14½pt by Post Typesetters
Printed in Australia by Alken Press Pty. Ltd, Smithfield

10 9 8 7 6 5 4 3 2
00 99 98 97

Distributed in the United States by:
    Morehouse Publishing
    PO Box 1321
    HARRISBURG PA 17105
    Ph: (1800) 877 0012
    Fax: (717) 541 8128

Distributed in Ireland and the U.K. by:
    Columba Book Service
    55A Spruce Avenue
    Stillorgan Industrial Park
    BLACKROCK CO. DUBLIN
    Ph: (01) 294 2556
    Fax: (01) 294 2564

Distributed in Canada by:
    Novalis
    49 Front Street East
    Second Floor
    TORONTO, ONT M5E 1B3
    Ph: (1800) 387 7164
    Fax: (416) 363 9409

Distributed in New Zealand by:
    Catholic Supplies (NZ) Ltd
    80 Adelaide Road
    WELLINGTON
    Ph: (04) 384 3665
    Fax: (04) 384 3663

Dedication

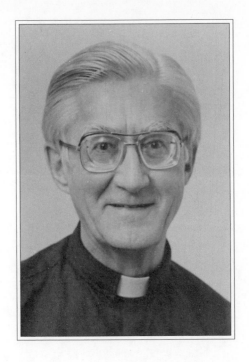

to Rev. Carroll Stuhlmueller, C.P.
1923–1994

•

*who loved and lived the Word of God
and inspired a multitude of students
and readers to do the same.*

Foreword

PAUL GLYNN HAS PRODUCED A LABOR OF LOVE, IF THERE EVER was one. Every page of this book on the psalms is testimony to the author's reverence and love for these great biblical prayers. And his love is infectious. All the while protesting that he is an amateur, Fr Glynn skilfully demonstrates the poetic depth of the psalms, their complex relationship to Israel's history, and the epic biblical themes that course through them. The reader who may just be beginning to get acquainted with this part of the Bible will find here an informed, sure footed, and spirited guide.

There is another love that shines through these pages— the author's love for his mentor on the psalms, Fr Carroll Stuhlmueller, C.P. This is a love that Paul Glynn and I share and another reason why I am honored to add a word of introduction to this engaging book. Carroll Stuhlmueller was a great biblical scholar and a magnificent teacher. Even more compelling, he was a lovable human being, an original whom no one could take for granted. I had the privilege of being Carroll's brother religious, teaching colleague, and good friend for many years. There wasn't one false note about him. All of his energy was dedicated to biblical scholarship and his genuine piety, profound sense of prayer, and humble goodness found their roots in the Bible as well.

In reading this book, I was touched by Paul Glynn's love

and respect for Carroll as the one who introduced him to a deeper understanding of the psalms. For many years, Carroll had taught both the prophets and the psalms, but toward the end of his life it was his course on the psalms that seemed to be the gathering place for all his experience and the deep wisdom of his soul. Every year, more and more students sought him out. Fittingly enough he was teaching a course on the psalms when God called him home.

Carroll, I know, would be pleased with this book. He would surely be touched by the words of praise that come his way on these pages, but even more pleased with the prospect that through this book many more people would drink anew from the wellsprings of the psalms.

Donald Senior, C.P.
Catholic Theological Union
Chicago, Illinois

Contents

Introduction

T HERE IS A STORY TOLD OF A PROFESSOR WHO MADE A remarkable breakthrough in the field of enzymes and was in
demand all over the land to lecture on his discovery. He
had a chauffeur who always drove him to those places that
were reasonably close, and who used to sit in the audience
for the lectures. The two enjoyed each other's company,
had become firm friends, and used to bet against each other
on baseball games and the like. One day the chauffeur said:
"I've heard that enzyme lecture so many times I could give
it myself." The professor replied: "Put your money where
your mouth is! I have to speak at a small country university
next week. I'll bet you $100 you can't do it."

So, off they went a week later, each dressed as the other.
The chauffeur ascended the stage and gave the lecture
word perfect, even writing the complicated equation on
the blackboard. The *tour de force* was concluding in a burst
of applause and the chauffeur's smiles when a local professor ran from the audience onto the stage and pleaded:
"Professor, I've struggled with a problem for years. Just let
me add another equation you know well." He took the
chalk and furiously wrote on the board.

"Professor, I know it's a difficult problem but how can
you reconcile the two formulas?"

The professor dressed up as the chauffeur enjoyed this
unexpected crisis for the pseudo-lecturer. The latter,

however, didn't bat an eyelid, but said with disdain: "Difficult? That's not difficult. I'll bet you $100 my chauffeur down there can solve your problem."

At Mass I wear a long white robe like Jesus and give off wisdom that all comes from him! I'm just like the chauffeur on the stage, and doubly so in this book on the psalms. Almost all I have to write comes from a mighty professor of Old Testament studies, the American Passionist priest Carroll Stuhlmueller. Famous among scholars for his books and contributions to biblical commentaries and journals, he is read and loved by many non-professionals for his six-book series, *Biblical Meditations* (on the Scripture texts used at Mass for every day of the year). He died of a massive stroke in 1994, mourned by a multitude of admirers.

But first, let us go back to 1947, the time I first began reading the psalms daily, when I entered the Marist Novitiate. It was situated on the outskirts of Armidale in the highlands of New South Wales, Australia. I was brought up on the river flats around Lismore and found the Armidale mountain air and scenery very stimulating. I also found the other 15 novices spiritually stimulating. Half had entered straight after graduating from high school and half were late vocations, including a lawyer, a policeman, a wool classer, and four who had been demobilized from the armed services a year or so before, following the ending of the Pacific War. The novitiate was physically and spiritually tough, but it became the happiest year I have ever experienced. We were mostly on total monastic silence and our main breaks from lengthy prayer and study were spent working outdoors on the extensive farm, gardens, and grounds. There was no radio, newspaper, or magazine, no alcohol and not a cent of spending money.

If the novice was unable to discover a companionship with the Lord, he would not last the unrelenting 365-day preparation for temporary vows and the seven-year seminary course. You could say the essential job of a priest or religious is tasting the Lord's companionship, and helping others to that energizing experience. Which was surely "the one thing necessary" that Martha was in danger of missing (Lk 10:41–42).

Novitiate was my real introduction to the psalms, which we chanted in the chapel a number of times each day. A small commentary by Irishwoman Mary Ryan whetted my appetite to understand these religious poems that have been and are wellsprings of prayer for countless millions. As with most great poetry, the psalms' meaning is not always clear, replete as they are with metaphors, allusions, symbols, and experiences often dating back several millennia. Ordained a priest seven years after my novitiate, I began praying the breviary, which includes about a dozen psalms daily. Over the next three decades I tried to understand the psalms better via books, tapes, and lectures, but I never felt quite satisfied. Then in the early eighties, Carroll Stuhlmueller came to Japan to give a summer school on the psalms. At the end of it I was telling myself: This is the teacher I've been looking for since 1947! I devoured his three books on the psalms and did his more extensive psalms course at Catholic Theological Union, Chicago. I gained so much from him that I decided I wanted to share some of his insights with people who were not in a position to study under him—and hopefully lead them to read his psalm books. He readily gave me permission to use anything he wrote or said. His great friend and publisher, Michael Glazier—who is also a great lover of the Bible—authorized me to quote from the Stuhlmueller books that he had published.

If you knew Carroll Stuhlmueller you would know how much spiritual energy the psalms gave him. He claimed they will give anyone energy who will take the time to study them and read them prayerfully. He loved to highlight a second promise: we will break out of the small and often suffocating world of "little me" if we learn to praise and thank the Lord in the spirit and words of the psalms. The beautiful "New Song" psalms, he said, teach us to put words to the melodies that pulsate through woods, fields, night skies, and seas—and echo in the human heart, though often in half-heard or even confusing notes.

There are many allusions in the psalms to a pre-Revelation concept of Israel's neighbors, the cosmic "Waters of Chaos." Stuhlmueller interprets this as the psalms' insistent call to join with God in fighting primeval yet ever present chaos (sin, fear, alienation, etc.), and in struggling to preserve his peace and order. Carroll Stuhlmueller staked his whole life on the truth of the Scriptures, but was in no sense a fundamentalist. He delighted in pointing out how the Holy Spirit used the insights of surrounding "pagans"—psalms 29 and 104, for instance, borrowed from the religious hymns of Canaan and Egypt. He often traced the "development of doctrine." For example, the earlier psalms portray life after death as the non-conscious twilight world of Sheol, even for the just; the idea of eternal life with God after death came to Israel late, about 165 BC.

Several years ago I asked a professor of a Old Testament in a prestigious Australian theological college: Who is the best modern commentator on the psalms? He replied without hesitation: "If you mean from a pastoral point of view, Stuhlmueller." He told me that by "pastoral" he meant what gave inspiration and personal spiritual help. I was delighted because that coincided with my own experience. Carroll would tell his students: "Scientific study of the words of the psalms must lead to the living Word, to prayerful communication with the Eternal Logos. Rational approaches, if authentic, lead to contemplative silence in his loving presence." However, he would add: "Contemplation must be of the true God, the One who is present in human life with its suffering and sin. Otherwise it runs the risk of becoming ecstatic deism or poetic trance."

The psalms inspired and energized Jesus—he quoted them often, far more than any other part of the Hebrew Scriptures. The same holds for many great disciples of Jesus—from the early Fathers, such as St Augustine, to moderns like St Thérèse of Lisieux and the second United Nations Secretary General, Dag Hammarksjöld. Stuhlmueller once said: "It is symbolic that the psalms are found in the middle of the Bible. They are its heart, and what the other books lead to—personal and communal ('liturgical') communication and loving relationship with the Lord." The man who inspired Augustine, Ambrose of Milan (who died in 397), wrote in his commentary on the psalms: "Although the whole of sacred Scripture breathes the spirit of God's grace, this is especially true of the delightful book of psalms . . . In the psalms there is something more than in the other books of Scripture: there is a kind of medicine for our spiritual health . . . a remedy for human passions. If you take the trouble to study them, the psalms become a gymnasium . . . a stadium of virtue with all manner of training exercises. You are able to choose the ones best suited to yourself . . ."

Like the Nazi-era martyr Dietrich Bonhoeffer, Stuhlmueller had little sympathy for "cheap grace." He insisted that the psalms demand responsibility, maturity, accountability, and the acceptance of darkness and pain as part of the human journey. He lectured with particular "authority" on the 50-odd psalms that are termed "Laments." Often powerful psychological studies of the contradictions, reversals, sufferings, and confusion that are willy-nilly companions on most human journeys, the Laments provide answers not found in Freudian text books. Stuhlmueller points out that they rarely give any rational answers—they simply bring the problems to the Lord and to the temple liturgy. Psalm 88 is surely the most terrible of the Laments. Stuhlmueller sees it as born of a crisis "when creed, ritual, and family tradition collapse before the onslaught of failure and suffering. All must at some stage wait in darkness like this psalmist, trusting in a God who is silent and seems absent"—Maybe, he added, "as a decrepit and shaking inmate of a retirement hospice. Statistics indicate more and more of us will end up like this." He continued: "If we have learned to trust like this psalmist, we will be able to bear with those diminishments and humiliations with serenity." He said this with deep emotion—he had just been visiting his once brilliant teacher Barnabas Ahern, who was eking out his days in the no-man's-land of Alzheimer's disease. Stuhlmueller concluded: "Psalm 88 ends with: 'My only friend is darkness'—shocking words, except for those who have learned to befriend the darkness as being as much a part of human life as winter is of nature's beneficent but sometimes demanding cycle."

Psalm 44 is another psalm parented by pain and distress. It questions God and runs dangerously close to accusing him of callous indifference to human suffering and even of breaking his promises. The psalmist's resentment finally boils over in verse 23. God is standing idle while faithful Israelites groan under foreign oppression: "Wake up! Why are you asleep Lord!" Stuhlmueller comments: "None of the questions are answered. Yet to speak them before God—and for them to become the word of God in the Bible—means that God and the people were communicating at a depth beyond words."

Stuhlmueller had a special love for the Pilgrim Psalms (Psalms 120–134, plus several others). They are full of journeys of the past that tell us much about our own wayfaring today. He loved Psalm 131, which he saw as the trustful confession of an old person who as an overconfident youth had planned to solve all problems and set the world on fire. "But now he has discovered humility and peace in the Lord and is freed of the old compulsive need to berate others." Psalm 123, written when the Israelites groaned under slavery to foreign masters, teaches believers to look beyond material circumstances to God, and to discover dignity and freedom of spirit in him. It is a timely psalm for many today who are captive to poverty, illness, broken families, or embittered relationships. The psalms show the way to discover meaning within apparent meaninglessness.

Psalm 78:2 promises "to reveal hidden lessons of the past." Stuhlmueller often brought up the dimension of "the history of salvation" in the psalms. The psalmists were not spiritual Lone Rangers—however appealing that romantic but ultimately anti-social idea might be to moderns fed a diet of fiction cooked by novelists and television producers who are often highly individualistic, self-centered, and unhappy in their own marriages and interpersonal lives. The psalms were born in communal temple liturgies that recited—and often re-enacted in song, dance, and gesture—God's salvation initiatives in Israel's history. Communal temple liturgies were the wellsprings of the psalms and the normal place to best experience their energy and spirituality. The same experience is available today in local parish liturgies—especially if preparation for these include private (or prayer-meeting) reading of the psalms.

Stuhlmueller frequently spent time explaining the original Hebrew and Aramaic words, for instance *rahamin*, a word appearing in many psalms. It has no English equivalent and is generally translated by "compassion," "mercy," or "pity." In fact, its literal Hebrew meaning is "the feeling of a mother for the child of her womb." Expounding on the implications of *rahamin* could move Stuhlmueller, and his class, close to tears! A mother does not feel pity or mercy for her child but love and pride. *Rahamin* tells us God feels this way toward us, with a divine determination to do all that is possible so that we develop the nobility that befits his children. As Deuteronomy 32 tells us, we were created by the Eagle God to be eagles—not chickens with beaks and eyes ever on the ground looking for scraps, even rotting ones! Stuhlmueller saw the human dimension of *rahamin* in the helplessness and darkness of the womb. The biblical call is for many deaths to old attitudes, prejudices, etc., and for rebirths to new and more authentic living. For Stuhlmueller, *rahamin* showed that it is all right to experience the darkness and feebleness of the womb again and again, because it is the womb of God.

A great message for modern parents, teachers, and priests was seen by Stuhlmueller in Psalm 73. It is the story of a temple official who almost gave up the faith, so abandoning his responsibility for the spiritual welfare of the young. The first part of the psalm outlines the fierce struggle to keep on the hard, narrow path when the wide, lush pastures of unbelievers called seductively. Bitterness and resentment at God's apparent disinterest or helplessness all but overwhelmed the psalmist. But then, the powerful verses 17 and 23–28! Peace and enthusiasm for the things of God have returned. As in numerous psalms and the Book of Job, no answers are given to the doubt-ridden questions. There is, however, a vibrant proclamation that all is well because the Lord holds the psalmist "by my right hand."

Stuhlmueller loved to trace the family tree of many psalms back to Exodus, Isaiah, Jeremiah, Job, and other parts of the Bible, etc. "O that TODAY you would hear his voice," Psalm 95:7, is one of the psalms that springs from Deuteronomy, a book full of "today." That book and the psalms are "no musty and outdated documents." They tell of ancient deeds but the Do-er is just as real and active today, here and now. He is the Lord of history, past and present. Stuhlmueller saw a touching example of this in Psalm 105:33. The Holy Spirit inspired the composer to change the original "flax and barley" of Exodus 9:31 to "grape vines and fig trees." The mighty deeds of the Lord who "blasted the flax and barley" of the slave-master Egyptians are happening right now in Israel, where the fields grow grapes and figs. What they remember of past history in Egyptian fields happens again, now, in the lives of the faithful in Israel.

Young students readily criticize their teachers, school, and the exam system—especially if their own marks are not too good! Organized religion is a kind of school system and critics have never been few. Many have good motives—after all Vatican II spoke of a Church ever in need of reforming. Be that as it may, the psalms are the prayers of a faithful that is temple-centered and institutionalized. Stuhlmueller, who was never loathe to criticize what he perceived as inauthentic, points to the great number of Zion and Temple Psalms as proof of that. The temple and, later, the Church are essential elements of biblical religion, as much as marriage and family are of human life.

A magnificent group of psalms is the Royal Messianic. Stuhlmueller did not see these psalms as straightforward, easily decipherable prophecies about Jesus of Nazareth. Peter did not come to believe Jesus was the Son of the living God by "flesh and blood" but through a "revelation from my Father in Heaven." Belief is God's gift not a clever human discovery. Belief in the coming Messiah was one of the essentials of the psalmists' faith. Stuhlmueller spent much time on the psalms concerning the Messiah. They portray him so gloriously that only a super-human person could fulfill them. Either a Priest-Prophet-King with divine attributes will come and reign or the Messianic Psalms are merely beautiful but wildly fanciful longings of lonely human hearts. In fact, Stuhlmueller found all the ideals and yearnings of his highly intellectual and warmly emotional self, extraordinarily fulfilled in Jesus of Nazareth, carpenter, Messiah, and Eternal Logos.

In this book I have followed the custom of the Jewish

composers of the psalms and written the Divine Name without the vowels, simply YHWH. The psalmists warned Israelites of the dangers of foreign, pagan domination—we face the danger of cocacolonization. American Indians were tricked into giving up their land for glittering beads—the neo-colonizers are not Americans as such, but materialists who can be found throughout the world. We moderns have been sold short, too, and now believe everything in life, including the Scriptures, should come cheap and tasty like hamburgers and French fries. Mystery and the transcendent are to be eschewed. Even God must be made buddy-buddy! But Stuhlmueller taught the Scriptural *El Shaddai*, the lofty Mountain God. He is the Eagle God Moses wrote of, not the chicken God, the domesticated, pen-bound God! Raymond Tournay and other modern scholars find it appropriate to combat this over-earthing of everything, including God, by using YHWH—lest in overreacting against the mistaken Lord of fear, we forget the Scriptures' many exhortations to a healthy fear of the Lord.

But enough of the ideas of this chauffeur in professor's gear. Let the wonderful passengers in my borrowed bus speak—Professors Stuhlmueller, Tournay, A. A. Anderson, Bernhard Anderson, *et alii*. They have spent a lifetime studying and praying the psalms. Their insights will help you, I feel sure, appreciate the psalms better.

The World's Favorite Psalm

Psalm 23

TEN-YEAR-OLD LUCY LOVED HER MOTHER AND USUALLY behaved herself. However, she also loved caramel tart, and was easily led into temptation one cold and rainy afternoon. Arriving home from school to a deserted house she discovered a note saying her mother would be back about 5 p.m. She also discovered a freshly baked caramel tart, cut into the right number of pieces for that night's dessert. Finding a sharp knife she carefully cut off narrow slices and gobbled them down ecstatically. Like a professional assassin she cleaned the knife. No one would notice.

But mothers do notice and Lucy's pretended ignorance made it worse. This particular mother was doing a course in sacramental symbolism with other parishioners on the liturgy committee. To show the "lying little glutton" that sin alienates the sinner from the community, her mother set a small table in the dining room where Lucy would be forced to sit alone during the family meal that night. Her siblings were told to ignore selfish Lucy absolutely.

This was a fervent family where mother or father read a snippet from the Bible at evening meals and special occasions. The parents would also nominate a child to say grace, spontaneous prayer being encouraged. Before the unusually stern-looking parents had a chance to select tonight's sayer of grace, Lucy closed her eyes, joined her hands reverently and said aloud: "The Lord is my shepherd, I shall not want. He hast prepared a table for me in the midst of mine enemies."

Did this really happen? I'm not sure, but it could have happened, so popular and well known is Psalm 23. Simple and beautiful like Beethoven's Pastoral Symphony it has won hearts for two and a half millennia. It has found its way into century upon century of literature. Ship captains in movies recite it at burials at sea, small children recite it at school liturgies.

The psalms are poetry, of course, songs born from what St Paul loves to call the spirit (*pneuma* in the Greek that Paul used), which he distinguishes from the lower faculty for knowing, the "psyche" (the soul or "rational intellect"). With the psyche we can study philosophy, mathematics, science, etc. With the *pneuma*, the spirit, we enjoy music and can create poetry. The psalms were born from the Spirit of God touching human spirits. As with all great poetry (and music and art), there are meanings within meanings and a variety of interpretations. I thought I was quite familiar with the poetry of Psalm 23 until I read Bernhard Anderson's book on the Psalms, *Out of the Depths*. I found myself choosing his interpretation because it gave me what the Japanese called "The Ah!" response—in interpreting, for instance, a haiku poem.

There are two distinct metaphors in Psalm 23, Anderson writes. First there is the simple and touching image of God as the faithful shepherd who guides the believer to nourishing pastures and good water. Like shepherds in old Israel he carries a stout staff to ward off wild beasts that sometimes crept up when darkness fell. You are familiar with this. But then comes an abrupt change of metaphor—for no shepherd sits his sheep down at table, nor anoints them with oil, nor fills a cup for them!

The latter metaphor comes from the customs of the desert Bedouin and their strict laws of receiving guests. When a Bedouin chief invites a stranger into his tent, has a meal served to him, and anoints his head with oil, that visitor is no longer a stranger. He is a member of the chieftain's clan while he remains with them. Anderson suggests that this custom, which the Israelites knew from their primitive Bedouin days, is the basis of the psalm's second section. The scenario is of a fugitive who rushes into a campsite of Bedouin tents and asks for asylum from his pursuers, hell-bent on violence and hot on his trail. The chieftain listens to his story, believes he is wrongly pursued and takes him into his tent. There the fugitive is given a meal and anointed with oil. That hospitality ritual symbolized acceptance into the clan. At this stage the enemies arrive and look on ("You prepare a table for me under the eyes of my enemies"). They know they will have to fight the chieftain and his whole tribe if they attempt to capture or harm their quarry. The Shepherd God who leads us through dark valleys to sustaining nourishment and refreshing water is also the Chieftain God who admits us into his tribe and who will fight on our side when enemies seek us out to destroy us.

All too primitive for the late twentieth century? No, this psalm surely has a saving message for our society, whose daily newspapers are full of cocaine deaths, ethnic wars, motor vehicle carnage, and broken homes. Our era's child prostitution rivals the worst excesses of primitive times or the relatively recent Roman Empire.

Historians also point out that in Imperial Rome there were more slaves than free citizens. What proportion of *our* citizens are truly free, free to be truly human? Many politicians are not free to resist bribes, nor journalists to resist sensationalism and rigged articles, nor priests and tele-evangelists to resist the temptations they preach against.

We, like our Jewish ancestors in faith, find freedom within a violent society when we find our way to the tent and clan of the Chieftain God. He will fight for us and teach us how to fight evil. He anoints us with the oil of covenant baptism, making us members of his people, and feeds us with his flesh and blood. We become what G. K. Chesterton calls in his great prophetic poem, "The Ballad of the White Horse," the fighters "who drink the blood of God." The setting of that poem is the Christian King Alfred's desperate wars to prevent the pagan Dane invaders destroying England's ninth-century Christian culture. But Chesterton's warning is also for today, when we are being attacked by the new Danes whose ranks include writers, film makers, journalists, and university professors:

> . . . men bound to Nothing, being slaves without a Lord,
>   By one blind idiot world obeyed, Too blind to be abhorred;
>   . . . By weird and weakness winning, Accursed from the beginning, By detail of the sinning, And denial of the sin;
>   By thought a crawling ruin, By life a leaping mire,
>   By a broken heart in the breast of the world, And the end of the world's desire . . .

Psalm 23 helps us fight with God for a human cosmos that is meaningful and loving.

2 *Sing a New Song*

Psalms 33, 40, 96, 144, 149
Is. 42:10
Rev. 5:9, 14:3

N OT ONLY FINNS BUT MUSIC LOVERS THE WORLD OVER HAIL "Finlandia" as a superb composition. Its composer Sibelius used to find his surest and deepest sources of musical inspiration in the unwritten symphonies of nature all around him. As a young man he would walk through the woods with a fiddle under his arm, delighted as he listened to bird songs, crickets, and the wind as it stirred, buffeted and caressed leaves and branches. Reaching a lake or quiet sea inlet, he would get into a boat and row to where the woods were close to the shoreline. He would first sit, simply taking in the sounds from the forest, the shoreline, and the sea. Then taking up his bow he would fiddle away spontaneously in reply to the music of his nature friends.

Most people can understand Sibelius' feelings as he did this. They too have been moved at the sound of wind soughing through a stand of she-oaks, or at the sight of the forest of stars in a cloudless night sky. The poet John of the Cross used the very apt phrase "silent music." Most of us from time to time have experienced a rich peace as we stood silent before nature in one of its myriad aspects.

Yes, most people hear this music, and the nations surrounding Israel heard it over that long period when the psalms were composed, amended, and gradually put into their final form. Yes, the surrounding nations wrote beautiful religious poetry about nature, but Carroll

Stuhlmueller writes: "Music and melody roll across the heavens and the earth, yet only Israel can put the proper words to it and transform the sweep of sound and melody of rhythm into 'a new song' for the Lord in the assembly of the faithful." God, whom the highest heavens cannot contain, dwells in a particular way at the Jerusalem Temple and in its psalm-oriented liturgies (Deut. 10:14–15).

The psalms contain revelation, a word coming from the Latin *revelare*, meaning to draw back the veil. God alone understands the meaning, size, duration, and future of the cosmos around us, and of the extraordinarily beautiful nature that clothes spaceship earth and, above all, the meaning and destiny of us humans. It is not just the "darks" around us and within us that veil ultimate meaning. We can, in the words of the Book of Wisdom (13:7), "strive to understand God's works and fall victim to appearances, dazzled by so much beauty." The mother points her finger at the full moon, repeating "moon, moon," but the infant only stares at the mother's finger. We are like slow-learning infants. God teaches us to see the moon and the meaning of the moon. Much of that teaching is via his revelations in the psalms.

One revelation that slowly unfolded in the psalms made the Israelite believers totally different from other believers throughout the world. The psalms gradually reveal One God who is the designer, creator, and motive force behind every aspect of nature. The abundant discoveries of archaeologists over the last two centuries provide clear pictures of the very different religious beliefs of the nations that surrounded Israel.

Canaanite, Ugaritic, Assyrian, Babylonian, and Egyptian inscriptions on stone, clay tablets, and papyrus, plus a wealth of idols and figurines show how these people worshipped a variety of gods as the controllers of the forces of nature. The sky and the rain were under the control of Baal, a god of the utmost importance to these agricultural people. Summer is rainless along the eastern shore of the Mediterranean. Priests and people would pray to Baal from late autumn, and when the vital winter rains began some-time around December they would shout and dance their thanks. If you have lived in Israel at this time of the year, you would probably have seen the spectacular lightning and thunder that usually precedes the breaking of the sum-mer drought. Believers in Baal saw the lightning flashes as his mighty javelins that split his enemies, and the mountain-shuddering thunderclaps as his voice. His worshippers called Baal "the Rider on the Clouds and the Lord of the Skies."

Asherah was the goddess of the sea. At a time when oceans claimed many victims, as well as precious mer-chandise, sailors and ship owners showed great devotion to her. Sometimes her statues carried a flower and a serpent. The flower (and her usually prominent breasts) signified the fertility she could bestow, while the serpent ominously pointed to the mystery of death. She was sometimes wor-shipped as "Queen of the heavens," the cult condemned in Jeremiah 44:17.

There was a goddess who rivalled Asherah's claims on fertility, Ishtar, known as "the Valiant Maiden." She was mistress of the arts of war and sexual love. Male believers would go to her shrines and have sex with her "sacred prostitutes" to ensure the fertility of their tribe, their fields, and their farm animals. But, like the serpent next to the flower on Asherah, there was fearful mystery in the cult of Ishtar. She sometimes had cruel and vicious moods that could only be appeased by blood. Those were the times when she caused terrible slaughter, even killing her own worshippers.

Mot was the feared god of the underworld. In the ancient past he had attacked Baal and killed him. That was the ultimate misfortune, for if Baal is dead there can be no clouds, no thunder and lightning, and no rain. Every living thing would die. But Ishtar loved Baal and she revenges him by killing Mot with a sword. Then, in words springing from the lips of people depending on the land: "With winnowing fan she winnows him, with fire she scorches him, with grain mill she grinds him. Then she scatters his seed in the fields." She carries Baal's body to the top of a sacred mountain and, through an elaborate rite of sacrifice, restores him to life. Baal rises joyfully, and hurls his shafts of lightning. Then with thunderous words he orders rain to fall. The dying fields lift up their heads because, like Lord Baal, they have received new life.

This poetic myth, deeply meaningful to the farmers of the ancient world, and which they believed actually happened every year, is found among peoples from the Mediterranean coast through to the sophisticated Babylonians in the far East. The yearly sickness unto death of the fields in winter and their rising with new life in spring terrified, fascinated, and thrilled not only farmers, but also townspeople, artisans, and kings. In worldly-wise Babylon, the Priest-King carried out yearly rites before the assembled clergy and courts that were seen as "sacramental"—religious signs that they believed actually accomplished nature's rising to new life, which was symbolized in the royal ritual.

Tiny Israel was surrounded, attacked, and often overwhelmed by armies from Egypt, Assyria, Babylon, Greece, and Rome. Not even averaging 100 kilometers from its eastern sea border to the west, where it was completely hemmed in by desert, Israel was the vital corridor of the fertile crescent that armies of the great powers must march along in the not infrequent wars. These conquering armies that contemptuously tramped over the Jews, attributed their power to their gods and goddesses: Baal, Asherah, Ishtar, Mot, and others. Tiny, ever-being-pushed-aside Israel—in that pre-Christian world where everyone else worshipped wonderful and often weird gods—alone worshiped the One God, the Creator of all. Surrounding nations, with the educational institutions, libraries, and travel opportunities that wealth makes possible, left impressive literature and religious poetry acclaiming the wonder and grandeur and mystery of the forces of nature. But the nations missed the main point that Israel had learned from YHWH's revelation: Nature's forces are not the manifestation of moody gods and goddesses. There is but one God, Creator of all, supremely compassionate, unfailingly a lover of goodness. The nations heard the mighty melodies in nature, but like an illiterate jungle dweller might listen to Beethoven's "Misa Solemnis." He would hear the music but not the meaning. That glorious "Et Homo Factus Est" ("And Was Made Man") may touch him with its stirring melody, but not energize him as it did the composer and the countless listeners who believe that God did become a man.

An example is Psalm 33:

Sing YHWH a New Song . . . by his word the heavens were made, all the heavenly bodies by his breath. He herds the seas into confines, holds the waters (of chaos) as in a bottle . . . He spoke and the world and all were made . . . From heaven he observes all people . . . He who made their hearts and knows all they do (vv. 3, 6, 7, 9, 13, 15).

This is the basic first line of the New Song—the One God who made the cosmos can see what goes on in the conscience of every person. But you see a more wonderful line of the New Song if you go back to verse 5: "And the earth is full of his HESED (steadfast, covenant love)."

Psalm 40:3 reads: "He has put a New Song on my lips." The psalmist's words race like a torrent as he enunciates the glorious lines of this New revealed Song: "Your wonders and plans are too many for us to count" (v. 5). Verse 11 extols YHWH's *hesed w'emet*, two covenant words appearing in dozens of the psalms. They mean God's steadfast love and his faithfulness to his promises.

Many centuries later, in the Greek of John's Gospel 1:14, the words came to be translated "grace and truth." The ancestors of so much in the New Testament are the psalms. The psalmist's New Song ends up with a *Kyrie Eleison*, "Lord have mercy," in verse 17. He knows he is "a wretch," but YHWH is his helper and his savior. This singing of the New Song is all the more wonderful in that it takes place while Solomon's Temple lies in ruins and the new temple has not yet been built (vv. 6–7). His trust in YHWH has stood the test of the Babylon debacle.

Psalm 149, which begins "Sing a New Song to the Lord" for "the Lord loves his people" (v. 4) continues with a somber "with high praises in their voices and two-edged swords in their hands" (v. 6). Scholars say the psalm is post-Babylon, when a weakened Israel had to struggle and fight forces bent on destroying the temple and the city again. Stuhlmueller points out that these clear lines of the New Song reveal that God's faithful believers must join him in the cosmic battle against evil. Believers in revelation cannot opt for neutrality in the ongoing war between goodness and evil.

The New Song in Psalm 144 (see v. 9) is very much a Good/Evil war song. YHWH "trains my hands for warfare . . . for battles . . . is my fortress . . . my shield (vv. 1–2). YHWH "Hurl your lightning . . . shoot your arrows, rout the enemy . . . deliver me from the deep waters (of chaos) . . . from alien foes whose mouths are full of lies, whose hands are raised in perjury" (vv. 6–8). Revelation is not a religion of soft options. You can't choose the beautiful parts about love and leave out the hard parts about struggle, sacrifice, and, at times, blood. Faithful Israelites were never long free from encroaching enemies who hated their temple and their worship of YHWH, and would cajole them with easy gods, cheap grace, temple prostitutes, and undemanding morality. The New Testament's last book, Revelation, speaks of the New Song too (5:9; 14:3)—and of the fierce persecutions the early Christians suffered. I think we would be fools to think ours is very different from the evil-laced societies of the Israelites of old or of the early Christians. We too can lose our faith and dilute revelation to ineffectiveness, if we are not prepared to fight as well as sing.

3 The Silent, Absent God

ONCE MET A JAPANESE ADULT WHO WAS STUDYING THE Gospels for the first time. He had been very attracted by Christ, hoping here might be the sure guide he had been seeking. Then he read the Passion Story and was shocked to see, he said, that Christ despaired on the Cross: "He cried out, My God, why have you deserted me?"

It was not a cry of despair. Christ in great pain of body and spirit cried aloud one of his favorite psalms. Christ obviously loved the Scriptures because he was continually quoting them. To each of the three temptations by Satan in the desert he replied with a quotation from Scripture. If you tally up his Scripture quotes you find that the psalms were the texts he quoted most of all. It is obvious that he loved these psalms, which brought such peace and energy. Christ lived 2000 years ago and was close to the culture and events that helped give birth to the psalms. One purpose of this book is to get readers more in touch with those same times and events, so as to share, to some extent, in Christ's love for the Psalms. To do so will include sharing in his gratitude to the faithful and heroic Jews who composed and preserved those psalms over the previous 1000 years of difficult and often turbulent history.

"My God, my God, why have you deserted me?" is the opening verse of Psalm 22. Stuhlmueller points out that this psalm is only fully understood against its historical context, the anarchic times of Jeremiah and Isaiah. In 597 BC, Babylon's colossal and merciless military arm seized Jerusalem and its leaders. Jewish resistance forces secretly built up and then revolted. In 587, the Babylonian army returned in great force and leveled the walls and city dwellings, and—unthinkable before it happened—destroyed the temple and altar and took off as booty the sacred Ark of the Covenant. No one knows the Ark's subsequent fate. Earlier psalms had promised that the line of Davidic kings would last forever. The Lord would protect them. The Jews fiercely believed these divine promises until Babylon gouged out the eyes of the last Davidic king to sit on a throne in Jerusalem. He died as a "felon" in a Mesopotamian dungeon, and no Zion throne would hold a Davidic successor.

The singers of Psalm 22 are totally confused and distraught at the Lord's seeming inability—or unwillingness?—to keep his promise of always protecting the temple and the Davidic line. They struggle to keep believing through the prolonged dark night. The Lord shows, it seems, not the slightest concern for them or the other faithful believers in the doomed city. Turncoats taunt them for their blind trust: "He trusted in the Lord, let him save him . . . if he really is his friend!" (v. 8). They pray on and trust desperately, but heaven appears as unfeeling as the metallic skies at the height of a terrible drought: "Lord, I call you all day and you give no reply. I pray to you all night but I get no peace" (v. 2).

Psalm 22 is one of a large number of psalms called Lamentations that struggle with pain. One third of the psalms are Lamentations which may be a commentary on the amount of pain in the lives of most people. Psalm 22 and some other Lamentation Psalms raise the old issue that Stuhlmueller calls "the problem of the silent, absent God." In the face of the horrendous pain in the hearts and bodies of Jews led off as slaves to distant Babylon, or to

their deaths in Auschwitz, or of Christians dying horren-
dously in the Colosseum, or of little children dying of sear-
ing bone cancer before the ravaged eyes of parents—is
God uncaring? Is he powerless to help, or—the blasphemous thought will not be silent—is he nonexistent? That
problem was no different in Jerusalem in the sixth-century
BC than it is in Sydney or New York as the year 2000
approaches!

Psalm 22:11b–15 cries out:

> I have no one to help me. A herd of bulls surrounds me,
> strong bulls . . . close in on me . . . like lions tearing and
> roaring. My being disappears like water draining away, my
> bones are wrenched from their sockets. My heart melts
> away like wax. My mouth is as parched as fired clay . . . A
> pack of dogs encircles me, a gang of ruffians closes in on
> me. They fasten my hands and feet and leave me lying in
> the dust of death . . . and they stand around me gloating.

Probably few of us have had experiences as terrifying as
the ones above. However many of us, if not the majority,
have gone through times of desolation when we can relate
to Psalm 22's: "My God, my God, why have you abandoned me?" As a priest I keep meeting Catholic parents
who with pain in their eyes initiate a discussion about
their sons and daughters. As long as the children were
minors they took them to Mass every Sunday, sent them to
Catholic schools, prayed with them in the home. Then
came graduation and the young adults stopped going to
church, saying they could "find no meaning in the Mass."
Next they set up house with a companion. Possibly preg-
nancy followed, but neither party spoke of marriage—"We
haven't decided if we will stay together." This almost
breaks the hearts of some parents. They have tried so
earnestly to bring up their children with robust Christian
faith. They spent so much time in prayer for them. And

now they say with Psalm 22: "I call you all day and you give no reply. I pray to you all night but I get no peace."

As Stuhlmueller comments on Psalm 22, the psalmist is going through a great trial where his faith in God seems in mortal danger. Those old Scripture passages, such as 1 Kings 8:23, that assured believers that God always shows great kindness to those who are faithful, suddenly seem meaningless or worse! Philosophical considerations and intellectual discussions with friends have not brought peace of heart, nor has giving vent to anger or bitterness. Now totally without confidence in himself or anyone else, the psalmist finally abandons himself unconditionally to God. He pleads with God to accept him as one of the *anawim*, the destitute poor whose only security is God. The word *anawim* (*ani* in the singular) began to appear frequently in the Bible after Babylon destroyed Jerusalem, the temple, and the Davidic line. The Jewish superiority complex that so angered the pre-Babylon Jeremiah and the writers of Isaiah gave way to near despair. Sometimes God has to allow hearts to break so that he can enter in, as Fulton Sheen used to say. The national calamity and consequent personal privations led the remnant *anawim* to a great deepening of faith and trust. It is a story repeated today.

When the psalmist made this act of abandonment to God's will, peace was born within the pain. Joy in worship returns (see vv. 22, 25). Pessimism about human life gives way to confidence: "The whole earth, from end to end, will remember and come back to the Lord" (v. 27). Doubts about the reliability of God's biblical revelations have dissipated: "My soul will live for him, my children will serve him . . . all this he has done" (vv. 30–31). Once again there is the experience that the words of the Bible contain more than their face value.

A young woman who died of tuberculosis in 1897, aged twenty-four had an extraordinary impact on the whole world through the only book she wrote, *The Story of a Soul*. And she only wrote that book because her Mother Prioress told her to. It would become France's best-seller after the Bible. This Thérèse Martin was a Carmelite and like her spiritual father, St John of the Cross, underwent a harrowing "dark night of the soul." Its intensity is glimpsed in a remark she made to her blood sister, also a Carmelite, some months before her death: "What a wonderful gift is the Faith. Without it I would have taken my own life!"

On another occasion, as youthful Mistress of Novices, she gave her charges a simple and profound formula for living the Christian life: "All you need to hold to are two dispositions of soul: abandonment to God's will, and gratitude." Her thinking wasn't very different from the composer(s) of Psalm Twenty-two, 2300 years before her. This unpretentious but often heroic spirituality can demand long waiting in the darkness for the silent, absent God. Sometimes the temptation arises that he is the great hoax, the nonexistent God. The experience in the latter part of Psalm 22, and in what was Thérèse's last will and testament, *The Story of a Soul*, gives ancient and modern testimony that he is very much the living God. And he is well worth waiting for in the darkness.

4 Hesed—
Steadfast Love

A JAPANESE FRIEND WROTE DOWN FOR ME A DOZEN DIFFERENT ways of saying "it is raining" in Japanese. Each of the expressions is evocative of the mood of nature accompanying each particular type of rainfall—whether it be an early spring drizzle, fierce thunderstorms at the end of a stifling summer day, gentle autumn rain, or the sodden rain of midwinter. I soon came to discover you need some knowledge of these nature-mood words if you are to appreciate Japan's nature-centered literature and especially classical haiku poetry.

Stuhlmueller, who often came to Japan to give summer schools and had some appreciation of Japanese poetry, pointed out a similar need if we are to understand the psalms properly—we must go back to the original and often unique Hebrew words. Secondly, we must never forget that the psalms teach through the medium of poetry. Poetry, he insisted, can often express the mysteries of human life and of God more surely than prose. Stuhlmueller would become very animated when he explained Hebrew words like *hesed*. The translators of the Bible into Greek, Latin, and English had no word of their own that fully expressed the Hebrew *hesed*, so they simply rendered it with words such as "love," "mercy," and "grace."

In the Bible *hesed* appears with that crucial intervention

of God into human history that revealed his choice of Israel as his very own people, his very own "tribe." Exodus 19:5 has it: ". . . you of all the nations shall be my very own." This divine choice is reiterated time and again in the Old Testament, assuring the Jews they are the Chosen People, covenanted and adopted as his own children.

The biblical Israelites had a very broad and deep concept of adoption. A child, or even an adult, adopted into a family became real kin, bonded as truly as if sharing the same blood. The Babylonians leveled Jerusalem and—to the Jews' disbelief—the temple in 587 BC. They then force marched the population to Babylon, over 1000 kilometers away. Though the Jews were stunned with shock that this could be happening, a solid core of them doggedly held on to the belief that they were God's Chosen People, his very own family. Somehow or other, God their Father would make it all right. We see this magnificent faith in some of the psalms. The Jews were completely subjugated by the all-conquering Babylonians, who fought under the protection of gods like Marduk, Lord of the gods; Hadad, god of storms and thunder; Ishtar, goddess of love and fertility; and Sin the Moon god. Far from cowering before the idols of these victor gods, the Jews ridiculed them in psalms like Psalm 115:5–8, mocking the idols of gods/goddesses who "have mouths but never speak, eyes but never see, ears but never hear." The trauma of the destruction of Jerusalem and the consequent Babylonian captivity (which became the historical matrix of much in the psalms) would purify, deepen, and spiritualize Jewish understanding of God's promises about the covenant with his Chosen People, about the royal Davidic line not dying out, and about the temple. Several of the Babylonian-influenced psalms are sad, even complaining that God is not true to his covenant. Such psalms speak to us moderns because pagan "Babylon" has breached our walls, invaded our homes, and even, it seems, some of our religious gatherings. Frequent media reports of ozone holes, polluted cities, and species dying-out introduce doubts about "the good earth" surviving. Widespread and often sanctioned promotion of immorality makes many wonder about the future of our race. Many ask today, as not a few Jews asked in Babylon, Where is God? Where is his providence? Is there a God?

However, let us return to the hopeful word *hesed*, used in many psalms in conjunction with God's covenant with the Jewish people. Stuhlmueller, in his two-volume commentary on the psalms, writes: "Steadfast love [*hesed*] denotes a close bond of blood and loyalty . . ." (*Psalms 2*, p. 63). In his *Biblical Meditations for Lent*, he writes: "When love . . . is genuine it exemplifies the deeper meaning of its Hebrew root, *hesed*. In Israel's culture *hesed* existed only in a family or clan or tribe, never between strangers or foreigners. When God declared himself a kinsman or blood relative of Israel, then the bond of such a relationship was rooted in God. All equally belonged to God and consequently to one another's family" (p. 50). Commenting on the extraordinary Psalm 136, Stuhlmueller notes the occurrence of *hesed* in every one of its 26 verses: "This word [*hesed*] implies a pledge or strong sense of loyalty and so is reducible to the former sense of blood kinship. The history of the universe and of the people of Israel develops from a bond of 'blood' or kinship between YHWH and this chosen nation" (*Psalms 2*, p. 185). In *hesed* psalm after *hesed* psalm, the Holy Spirit tells the Jews that the Father has made them his own kin.

Psalm 136 begins: "Give thanks to the Lord for he is good, his steadfast love (*hesed*) endures forever." In the following 25 verses, the psalm gives an overview of history, beginning with the creation of the cosmos and moving through the great events of salvation in Israel's history. At the end of every verse is the assurance that these good things have happened "because his steadfast love (*hesed*) endures forever." The *hesed* blood relationship that

YHWH has made with the Chosen People actually flows out to the whole world and all its inhabitants: "He provides for all living creatures, his steadfast love (*hesed*) lasts forever." The psalmist has a vision similar to that of St Francis—the Holy Spirit led the Poor Man of Assisi to see that the universal Fatherhood of God gave him a kinship with all creatures. So he burst into his Canticle of the Sun, praising and rejoicing with Brother Sun and Sister Moon, Brother Fire and Sister Water.

God's *hesed* love for the Jews runs through the book of Psalms. Psalm 5:7 says: "But I, because of your great steadfast love (*hesed*), may enter your house, bowing down in your temple, reverencing you." Many psalms thrill with this feeling of familiarity, of literally being at home in "your house" (the Jerusalem temple). The composers of the psalms understood the implications of God's *hesed* love for Israel. Very often joyful and exuberant, they call on fellow Jews to clap hands, dance, sing, shout, and exult.

You may wish to read for yourself some *hesed*-love psalms. One note of caution: some old Bibles number the psalms in a way that is different to modern versions; the number of the psalm can be different by one. For example, Psalm 50 in modern Bibles is Psalm 49 in some old Bibles, Psalm 92 is Psalm 91, etc. Sometimes you will find that the psalms will be numbered Psalm 91 (92), indicating that Psalm 91 in the old numbering is now Psalm 92 in modern versions. Verse numbering can sometimes differ slightly, too.

If you look up these texts in the *Jerusalem Bible*, one of the outstanding modern translations, you will note that the translation for *hesed* love is "faithful love." So, on to some *hesed* references in the psalms: 6:4; 25:6; 26:3; 36:7; 40:10–11; 44:26; 48:9; 51:1; 57:10; 59:17; 61:7; 62:12; 66:20; 69:16; 85:7,10; 86:5,13; 88:11; 89:1,2,14,24,33,49; 90:14; 92:2; 94:18; 100:5 (v. 3 says "we are his people, the flock he pastures"); 101:1; 103:4,8,11;17; 106:1; 107:8,15,

21,31,43; 108:4; 109:26; 115:1; 117:2; 118:1,2,3,4,29; 119:41,64; 130:7; 136 (*hesed* love appears in each of its 26 verses as the motive force of God's work in nature and of his salvation deeds for his people, the Israelites); 138:2,8; 143:8,12; 144:2; 145:8,17; and 147:11. I've probably missed a few, but the above list certainly indicates that God's *hesed* love is of vital importance in the psalms, the key book of Israel at prayer.

God's *hesed* covenant with Moses made the Jews his Chosen People, God's very own family, but there are hints in several psalms that "the nations," the Gentiles, will be invited into this *hesed* covenant. Texts such as psalms 67:4–5 call on "the nations" to praise the Lord. Psalm 87 says Egypt, Babylon, Philistia, Tyre, and Ethiopia will come to acknowledge the Lord and gain entrance to Zion. Isaiah 2:1–3 has "all the nations" streaming to Jerusalem, where the Lord will teach them his ways. Isaiah 19:25 speaks of "my people Egypt, Assyria my creation, and Israel my inheritance." Isaiah 60:1–14, familiar to our ears from Christmas liturgies, has "the nations" coming to the Lord's light.

The post-Resurrection Jesus sent the apostles out "to all nations." Paul of Tarsus was the one *par excellence* to grasp this, and to go out and preach to non-Jews. He declared the walls of division between Jew and Gentile were broken down. All peoples were called to join the *hesed* covenant with God. He even calls the Son of God "our eldest brother."

5 Babylon, Auschwitz and God's Broken Promises

AS I WRITE THIS, IT IS JANUARY 27, THE ANNIVERSARY OF THE day the gates of the strange-smelling Auschwitz were flung open by Russian troops in 1945. A feeble "remnant" staggered out to freedom—but, alas, a freedom that would be limited for most by ever-restless memories. One would be heartless to lecture these dwindling survivors about forgetting what happened 50 years ago. Auschwitz was so horrendous that it is still as present to them as their wrist tattoos.

If modern Jews cannot forget the Nazi extermination program, neither could their ancestors, the psalmists, forget Babylon. By 597 BC, Nebuchadnezzar, Babylon's warrior king, had bloodily defeated all opposition—Assyria, Egypt, and the latter's ally Judah, setting up a puppet Davidic king, Zedechiah, in Jerusalem. Against Isaiah's warnings, Zedechiah joined Egypt in a conspiracy against the Babylonians. Nebuchadnezzar descended like a wolf on the Jerusalem fold, breaching the walls and sending in his troops to destroy and loot. The palace was razed and— the unthinkable blasphemy—the Temple of YHWH was leveled and its sacred vessels heaped up on carts of booty headed for Babylon. Then the Nazi-like decree: Every Jew the length and breadth of Judah, except those who were so sickly or feeble as to be a burden to the Babylonians, was to be rounded up—to be force marched to Babylon, well over 1000 kilometers of desert away. So began the 70-odd years of captivity in pagan Babylon.

This created a crisis of faith for Jews. They had believed the biblical assurances that the Holy City and its temple would stand forever. The people had read and sung God's assurances until they were essential parts of the Jewish faith. Psalm 48:8 glorifies ". . . this city of the Lord . . . which he has set up forever." Zion (sometimes called Sion) was the mountain outcrop in Jerusalem on which the temple and the Davidic-line palace were built. Psalm 68:16 says Mt Zion is the very "mountain of God where YHWH himself will dwell for all time." Psalm 125:1–2 glorifies this Mt. Zion as "immovable, there forever. Mountains ring Jerusalem, just as the Lord is a guard around his people, now and for all time." Psalm 76 promises that YHWH will always destroy enemies of the Jewish race because in Salem (an ancient name for Jerusalem) "is his home, he lives in Zion." The great Old Testament scholar, Bernhard W. Anderson, who lived and breathed the psalms, writes that their recitation convinced believing Jews that Jerusalem was "the city of YHWH, the very focus of his dwelling place on earth." So, to these Jews the destroyer of Jerusalem would have to be more powerful than YHWH! Or, equally blasphemous, the destruction of Jerusalem and the temple would mean that YHWH had made a solemn promise, a covenant that he could not keep! It was a problem for faith of major proportions.

Another spiritual crisis arose from the Babylon captivity: psalm after psalm had assured YHWH's people that he would keep Jerusalem's line of Davidic kings forever. Psalm 89:33–37 puts it: "I will never withdraw my love for him [the Davidic king] or fail in my faithfulness. I will not break my covenant, nor renege on my given word . . . His dynasty will last forever, his throne as visible as the sun, as everlasting as the moon." This is but one of many psalms enshrining YHWH's oath about the Davidic line ruling forever. Babylon gave the lie to that! The last Davidic king to sit on the Jerusalem throne and truly rule was Zedechiah. In 587 BC the Babylonians took Jerusalem for a second time, and leveled every building of importance, concentrating on places specially associated with the Jewish leader. King Zedechiah was bound, had his eyes gouged out, and was carted off to Babylon where he died in a dungeon. Many Jewish exiles in Babylon stopped praying the psalms—they stuck in their throats! This is when new questions, like "Where is your God, your vaunted YHWH?" begin to creep into some of the psalms, like a spreading cancer in the faith of dying Israel.

Auschwitz is a modern Babylon and the problem of God's broken promises became a personal one for me when I sat in the wrong seat on a plane going to Israel, a quarter of a century ago. "You're in my seat but it doesn't matter, Father," said a vivacious but somewhat troubled-looking Hungarian Jewess, Magda. She had lost her trust in YHWH while an inmate of Auschwitz and was heading for Israel forlornly hoping to rediscover a faith in the Bible that had once been precious to her. Her belief broke down the day a Nazi guard had escorted Magda, then 26 years old and known as Inmate No. A9580, and told her: "Take a long look at that chimney smoke. It's the last of your mother and sister!" Magda knew I was a priest from my clerical collar and said with eyes hurting from pain and questioning: "Father, we prayed to him and he didn't hear us!" As a child and young woman she had prayed the psalms with her mother and sister, but on the cutting edge of Auschwitz his great promises became as tattered and shameful as their clothing. She asked me to pray for her because she longed to believe as she had in her youth. We parted at Tel Aviv. I went to Ain Karim to study St John's Gospel with Donald Senior, and then went on to study the psalms under Carroll Stuhlmueller at Chicago's Catholic Theological Union. Part of my course was a detailed study of Europe's, especially Catholics' persecution of the Jews, which left me stunned. It greatly sharpened Magda's plea to "try to understand what we Jews have been through." A rabbi, Hayim Pereluter, was on the permanent C.T.U. teaching staff, a continual reminder of my promise to pray for Magda and to "try to understand."

I began to correspond with her, which led to a great respect for her and to a warm friendship. She wrote that after Tel Aviv she went to the old Wailing Wall, and "howled and howled" to YHWH. A terrible knot broke in her heart and she found herself talking to him again.

There is an expression that occurs in many Psalms, "to see his face." Scholars tell us its origin is in a religious custom of the surrounding "pagans." The statues of their temple gods remained covered until the climax of the liturgy, when the cloths were removed so that the worshipers could see the faces of their gods. As G. K. Chesterton used to point out, many pre-biblical customs show deep yearnings of the honest human heart, yearnings that would be fulfilled in the Holy Spirit's unique revelations through the Scriptures. The imaginative poets who composed the psalms borrowed "pagan" metaphors, including "to see God's face," to express their own spiritual longings and experiences. "To see his face" became the accepted liturgical expression for the very essence of true temple worship: the personal experience of the living, active YHWH, lovingly responding to sincere worshipers. Without that personal experience, worship and liturgy were really meaningless. The psalms formed a major part of temple liturgy so it is not surprising that expressions such as "to see his face" and "to seek his face" occur very often. See, for example, Psalms 11:7; 17:15; 22:24; 27:8–9; 42:2; and 105:4.

The dispirited Jews who were herded off to Babylon in 597 BC felt they were lost souls. The Jerusalem Temple, the sacred place where they had been able "to see His face" was gone. Had their past religious experiences in temple worship been mere illusion? Some tried to recite the psalms in alien Babylon but whole verses stuck like bones in their throats—those promises and oaths they had believed so simplistically about Zion, the temple, and the Davidic line standing forever! Some Jews refused to join in praying the psalms, their dejected spirits wincing as the pagans taunted the remnant of faithful believers with "Where now is your God?" (Pss. 10:4; 14:1; 22:8; etc.) But a committed group of believers in Babylon kept coming together to recite the psalms. And something new began to happen. Tournay, who wrote that great book *Seeing and Hearing God with the Psalms*, has described that "something new" very well.

I met Professor Raymond Tournay O.P. at Jerusalem's prestigious *Ecole Biblique*. In his native France during World War II, he had led a dangerous life helping Jews on the run. When I met him in Jerusalem in the early 1990s he was helping Palestinian civilians forced to live in appalling camps after armed Israelis had confiscated their generations-old homes. The Israeli authorities noted his activities with anger. My estimation of Tournay went up when I heard all of this from one of his fellow professors. What better man to teach the psalms than a world-class Old Testament scholar who has put his life on the line to live one of the key messages of the psalms: God's special compassion for the poor and oppressed, the *anawim* in Nazi-occupied France, and now in Israel.

Tournay has made a lifetime's study, in the original languages, of the historical/religious/cultural events that gradually gave the psalms their present form. He writes of the Babylonian captivity as a catastrophic flood, a kind of second deluge, that became the watershed of a deep, new spirituality. The dirty eastern waters in spate had submerged Jerusalem and every Judean town and village, but left behind plains and valleys rich in silt. After the veritable Waters of Chaos had subsided the fields began to glitter with spiritual crops bearing rich grain—the books of Isaiah and Jeremiah, and history's greatest collection of prayer poetry, the psalms.

Tournay pictures the pathetic scene early in the Babylonian captivity. Groups of faithful, if dispirited, Jewish priests, cantors, acolytes, etc., began to gather in one anothers' homes and recite the psalms. Not all would come, arguing that it was pointless to chant the psalms when their very heart, the Jerusalem temple liturgy, had stopped beating. Pathetic Psalm 137 alludes to this: "By the rivers of Babylon we sat and wept at the memory of Zion, hanging our harps on the poplars. We had been asked to sing one of YHWH's songs [psalms] to please our captors . . . How could we, in a pagan land?" But the ones who did come together to sing YHWH's praises began to experience something wonderful and new. Tournay calls it a "cultic theophany." Theophany means God making his presence felt and this was experienced in the temple-less cult or liturgy. YHWH had followed his people to this alien land, as Ezechiel would put it. The locus of his special presence on earth was no longer Jerusalem but Babylon, where Jews gathered for liturgical worship consisting mainly of reciting the psalms. Something like Chesterton's fantastic *Flying Inn*, the Jerusalem temple had risen from the ashes, taken wing, and come to Babylon.

6 More to Peter than Flesh and Blood!

'MY ENEMIES SAY TO ME THE DAY LONG: 'WHERE IS YOUR GOD?'' (Ps 42:11). I pray this kind of psalm better when I remember that Jews were taunted in Babylon with these words. It must have seemed that the taunts were spot on. The Babylonian gods had demonstrated that "the one, all powerful Creator YHWH, who is ever faithful to his very own covenanted people," was a phoney! We pray the psalms better when we get in touch with the historical situations in which the psalms were composed, or later rewritten. ("Redaction" is the term biblical experts use for such rewriting; it too was guided by the Holy Spirit.) There is only one way I know of getting to know the psalms' historical situations, the technical biblical metaphors (like "seeing his face"), the specifically Jewish words like *rahamin* and *hesed*, etc. That one way is to get hold of a good psalm-by-psalm commentary and carefully go through it. We all enjoy watching a football game much better if we know something of the names, faces, and past performances of at least the team we barrack for. Conversation can be dull with people too old to follow the news, or with recent migrants who don't speak our language. The psalms can be dull companions too if you know little of their "language." Anyone prepared to give to studying the psalms a fraction of the time they give to newspapers and radio broadcasts can learn the essentials of their idioms.

Reliable commentaries on the psalms abound. For instance, I have found to be very helpful the two-volume study by the Protestant scholar A. A. Anderson, of Manchester University, in "The New Century Bible Commentary" series. But the top of my hit parade remains the work of Carroll Stuhlmueller. Living for a time in the same building as him, while studying under him at Catholic Theological Union in Chicago, I came to see that he lived what he taught. He gave a wonderful lecture on Psalm 63. It is a moving psalm that shifts from anguish ("my body pines and my soul thirsts for you like parched earth does for water") to ecstatic happiness ("I have seen you in the temple . . . seen your glory. Your love is better than life . . . I will bless you while I have life . . . Lifting up my hands to you in praise . . . my soul wholly satisfied and my mouth praising you joyfully"). Stuhlmueller commented:

> "We need to lay aside significant time to pray, giving ourselves and the Lord sufficient time to gather our scattered wits. If we learn to pray seriously we will gradually experience this psalmist's thirst for spiritual, lasting things . . . and safely pass through the experience, which can be painful and even desperate, of seeing uncovered the selfishness and shallowness we had been cleverly hiding from others and even ourselves. This is the prelude, the condition of the psalmist's vision of God that becomes "a greater good than life."

Stuhlmueller warned us that we would not experience the living, energizing God of the psalms unless we are people of prayer. Living in the same building as Stuhlmueller during that three-month course, I discovered, I think, why he could convince, encourage, and fire with enthusiasm the hundreds enrolled in his course—he spoke from personal experience. If I got myself to the chapel by about

6.20 a.m. most mornings, he would be there. On one occasion I even sat a little side-on to C.T.U.'s most popular and prestigious writer and lecturer, and watched his face as he slowly read the psalms from his breviary. St Thomas Aquinas writes of how the Holy Spirit will teach the seeker to "relish" the words of Scripture. Stuhlmueller struck me as a living witness to that.

The highly influential Scripture commentator Origen, born in Egypt around 250 AD regarded St John's Gospel as the quintessence of the Bible. But he said you will understand it only "if you lean your head on Jesus' breast," as did the disciple John at the Last Supper—in other words, if you listen to Jesus and his Father in prayer. That's the condition for understanding and "relishing" the psalms.

The seventeenth-century scientist, mathematician, philosopher, and believer Blaise Pascal says in the book that became and remains a classic, *Pensées*: If you find anything of value in these pages know they come from a man who goes down on his knees. Another Frenchman, who has to win the Nobel Prize for medicine, Professor Alexis Carrel of the Lyons Medical University, went to the shrine of Our Lady of Lourdes as an unbeliever and ex-Catholic, to study "psychological improvements in health that are easily explained by the mass hysteria accompanying emotional demonstrations of faith." That's what he said when he met at Lourdes a fellow student from their medical university days. He added: "If a truly organic cure took place, that would be different. If Marie Ferrand was cured I would believe. But she will not be!" The woman had been in the same compartment of the Lourdes pilgrims' train that Carrel had traveled in from Paris. She was in the last stages of tubercular peritonitis, the hard mass of fluid in her stomach bulging ominously. Several times on the train journey she passed out and Carrel had given her morphine injections. He angrily jotted in his notebook that religion became fanaticism when it dragged dying patients like

Ferrand halfway across France in the heat of midsummer—only for them to die in greater misery! At Lourdes he tried unsuccessfully to prevent the unconscious woman being taken to the outdoor blessing of the sick. By now half-dead, she was carried to the procession, the bishop blessed her with the Eucharist, and Carrel thought the hot sun was playing tricks with his eyesight! The death pallor had left her face! When the swollen stomach flattened out, he later wrote, he thought he was going mad. He accompanied Ferrand back to the hospital, where several other doctors examined her carefully and declared that the pathetic patient of several hours before was now cured.

Carrel had witnessed a physical miracle, the very one he said could not happen, but he "still could not believe." He walked alone for hours, struggling with his dilemma. He argued with himself that maybe there was something in the air at Lourdes that could be responsible for the cure, as yet unknown to science. No, he realized, that's rubbish! No hitherto unknown substance could selectively cure just one of the crowd, turning scientific laws of medicine topsy-turvy in the process. Was some other explanation possible then? His mind and emotions thrashed about without rest.

Now it was late at night, and Carrel was as confused as when he first saw the woman physically transformed. A group of Basque pilgrims passed him singing to the Virgin and entered the Rosary Basilica. He too entered the church and sat on a chair at the back. For the first time since school days, he prayed. "Gentle Virgin . . . take unto Thyself this uneasy sinner with the troubled heart . . . and intellectual pride . . . who has a dream of believing in Thee and of loving Thee with the shining spirit of the men of God." He walked out into the night, "absorbed in prayer." Eventually returning to his hotel room, Carrel took out his notebook and concluded his observations. "All preoccupations with hypotheses, theories, and intellectual doubts have vanished ... Beneath the Holy Virgin's hand ... certitude." It was now 3 a.m., he writes, and, enfolded in a peace that banished doubt, he slept like a child.

Carrel wrote that in 1903. In 1912 he was awarded the Nobel Prize for discovering new ways of suturing blood vessels and transplanting organs. His experience at Lourdes is told in his slim volume, *Journey to Lourdes*, a book that soon went into many languages.

Dr Carrel made no progress in the ancient human dilemma—Is the supernatural real?—until he prayed with a real desire to know, and with humility. God, through Mary, solved his dilemma. When Peter was the first disciple to proclaim that Jesus was the Son of God (Mt. 16:13–17), the Lord replied: "... Happy Simon Peter! It was not flesh and blood [i.e. human thinking and cleverness] that revealed this to you, but my Father in heaven." God reveals himself; we don't figure him all out ourselves, anymore than the enclosed embryo figures out its mother.

Pascal adds a dark warning: "There is enough light for those who desire only to see, and enough darkness for those of a contrary disposition." Those words from *Pensées* rocked the famous Dr Nagai of Nagasaki. He was a convinced atheist until his mother's death shook his confident denials of the supernatural and of life after death. Then he began a four-and-a-half year study of Christianity, but "did not want to come to any conclusion just yet." He was a rising star and X-ray pioneer in Nagasaki's government university. It was 1937, when the militarist-controlled government was very anti-Christian. Baptism could endanger promotion, or even his job. He admits he was dilly-dallying with his conscience until Pascal's blunt words about "enough darkness" shocked him into action. Going humbly to the Nagasaki cathedral he enrolled in a course on the Gospels, and eventually received baptism. Eight years later he became the medical man of the moment when the atomic bomb hit Nagasaki, led a relief team of doctors and nurses for three months, and was one of a team who wrote the world's first scientific account of what an A-bomb does to its victims. Bedridden with radiation disease soon after that, widowed, and slowly and painfully dying, Nagai began writing the first of sixteen popular books that gave hope to millions of demoralized Japanese. A number of Nagai's books became national best sellers. Two were turned into classic movies that stirred the nation. The Tokyo Diet passed a bill in December 1949 making him a National Living Hero. He died in 1951, one of the most famous and loved men in the land. Many believe Nagai will one day be canonized. In his books he writes of his own super-confident atheist days and of how he came to find God only when he heeded Pascal's advice: Go down on your knees as well as sit at your study desk! "Go to Mass, even though you don't yet fully understand what it's all about," was another piece from Pascal that proved to be a milestone on Dr Nagai's long journey to a faith that he recognized was ultimately a gift from God.

Evagrius of Pontus, the theologian whose writings on climbing spiritual mountains greatly influenced Christianity's first monks and nuns, died in Egypt in 399 AD. Like many theologians who were writing in the period when the deadly persecution of Christians were not long over, Evagrius called a spade a spade. He had little time for people who taught Christianity without spending a lot of time praying. "A theologian is one whose prayer is true," he wrote. In other words, if you want to get your theology (or Bible interpretation) right, get your praying right! Wise advice for today, when all kinds of spiritual gurus, traveling medicine men/women, and spiritual snake-oil salespersons are on the go! So many moderns are leading "lives of quiet desperation" (Henry David Thoreau), that in panic they will give anyone a hearing. It is most unfortunate if that "anyone" happens to be teaching a shallow version of the religion revealed by God in the Bible. We have seen any number of lay people, clerics, and nuns, thundering away righteously in the media about what's wrong with the Church, only to give away their faith, priesthood, or religious life a few years later. Abbot David Gaerets OSB once remarked: "You can only survive as an angry prophet for the faith if you are prepared to do much prayer and fasting!" It is not all that hard to make a fair livelihood teaching theology and spirituality today, especially if you get a degree or two (which is also not all that hard these days). The danger is of ending up promoting yourself—even of selling religion—and, as Jesus warned, that can lead to selling your own soul, both in this world and the next. People who "use" the Bible are playing with fire—even hellfire, as Paul, Peter, and John warned in their epistles to the early Christians, some of whom were already teaching soft-option versions of the Gospel.

Most Catholics have been rocked, these last few years, by convictions in courts of priests and brothers who have sexually abused young people. Thanks be to God, I have not heard of any cases involving nuns, but several years ago I read a sad article in a prestigious magazine for Religious, about some nuns logging up thousands of miles, giving talks on poverty, all the while wearing Gucci clothing! I've also read articles in the secular media by nuns (and priests) attacking the old ways, and modern Church and state authorities. I sensed there was something very amiss in the articles, those all-important fruits of the Holy Spirit, enumerated in Galatians 5:22 being sadly lacking: "love, joy, peace, patience, kindness, goodness, trustfulness, gentleness, and self-control." In verse 19, Paul contrasts these attractive virtues with the fruits of self-indulgence, including "feuds and wrangling . . . bad temper and quarrels, disagreements, factions." My experience, with myself and in listening to others as a priest, is that we all have a nasty streak ready to break out and attack. The nuns and brothers who taught us called it Original Sin, while Japanese Buddhists speak of *Gu*—a mysterious word and concept—but we all experience its reality, leading to what Paul called "the fruits of self-indulgence." Jesus could continue his difficult voyages against the tide, often in the teeth of gales and storms, only by continually leaving the crowds, his preaching, and even his disciples to be alone with the Father. He took his frustrations, thwarted plans, and bruised heart to Abba. Refreshed by deep prayer, Jesus would return energetically to the crowds, and to "his own" who so often misunderstood and sometimes let him down. If we want to be disciples of the Gospel Jesus, we must often pray alone to the Father. If, unlike Jesus, we don't often take time out for prayer, but insist that we understand the mysteries of the Gospels, even presuming to lecture on spirituality and prayer, we might be in danger of hearing, in this world or the next, Jesus' shocking rebuke to the latterly promoted Simon, now officially the Rock: "Get out of my sight, Satan. You are a hindrance because you do not think as God does, but in the way of human flesh" (Mt 16:23). We will only meet the Father as Jesus did if we pray. We will only meet God in the psalms as Jesus did if we pray them. Jesus certainly was sustained and energized by them. He quotes them more than any other part of the Old Testament. As we have noted earlier, among the sparse sentences Jesus uttered while hanging crucified between heaven and earth, are verses from the psalms that arose spontaneously to his lips: "My God, my God, why have you forsaken me?" (Ps 22:1, recorded in Mt 27:47; Mk 15:34). In Luke 23:46, as his life seemed to flow away as meaninglessly as a gentle but hopeless rainfall on the desert sands, Jesus identified himself with the *ani*, the poor one of Psalm 31:5, and murmured: "Into your hands I commend my spirit."

My brother Tony, who spent nearly 42 years as a missionary in Japan, complained that the psalms he recited daily contained too many lines that he did not understand. He urged me, sometimes with impatience, to get on with this book on the psalms and finish it. He wrote to me, in May 1994, straight after the doctor's verdict that melanoma cancer was now in both lungs and death was only a matter of time. He admitted shock and disappointment. He and so many had prayed for a cure. "Why me?" kept rising in his thoughts, he wrote. At age sixty-eight, he was still vigorous, and had many plans underway for God's kingdom of love on earth. But the tone of his letter suddenly changed as those final words of Christ came into his mind: "Into your hands I commend my spirit." Tony wrote that he had begun repeating those words over and over in the darkness, and that a kind of new dawn had flooded his dark valley of disappointment, frustration, anger, and fear.

Tony had kept on praying the psalms each day as they appeared in his priest's breviary. Though he complained he failed to understand a great deal in the psalms, he kept on praying them. One result: Psalm 31 came to stay with him as his companion on the last journey, leading him home like Francis of Assisi's Sister Death—the eldest sister sent by the good Father to show her little brother the way through the last dark mile.

He encouraged me often and strongly to finish this book on the psalms. Tony said it would help priests, religious, and lay people pray the psalms better. When his death drew near and I went to be with him in Japan, he asked me sharply why I had not finished the book. I replied: "The psalms are so immense that I no sooner finish a chapter than I know it to be quite inadequate." No matter, Tony replied, every bit of writing about the psalms will help a few more people pray them better. He extracted my promise that, inadequate though it be, my book would be finished before he is dead a year!

7 Rahamin— and Stuhlmueller's Shivers of Emotion

TENKO NISHIDA BECAME VERY FAMOUS IN JAPAN LONG BEFORE his death in Kyoto in 1968, aged ninety-six. As a brash young man he was certain he had a sure-fire plan to make a lot of money. He talked a group of businessmen into putting up the capital and escorted one hundred farming households up to Japan's last frontier, the far northern island of Hokkaido, to begin a cooperative. That was in 1892. But everything went wrong. Cooperation went sour, debts increased, and capital was withdrawn. Everyone lost out. Tenko returned penniless and deflated to his Nagahama hometown, about 60 kilometers north-east of Kyoto. He was so disillusioned with people and himself that he made a drastic decision: he would enter an austere Buddhist monastery where he would fast and pray until he understood the purpose of life and found peace of heart.

Day after day he sat meditating in the severe lotus position on the hard *tatami* floor, but seemingly getting nowhere. On the most fateful day of his life he became distracted from his meditation by sounds outside that easily penetrated the *shooji*, the paper sliding window. It was obviously a woman with a howling baby, and the woman stopped just near his window, trying to soothe away the infant's tears and fears, but without success. Then Tenko heard the mother speak with great tenderness: "Ah, my tiny one, I know what you are crying for, you're hungry. Here is my breast, little one."

Tenko heard the crying stop and, as the contented child sucked sustenance from her breast, the mother happily hummed a soothing tune, so delighted was she to give the child of her own body. An extraordinary thing happened to Tenko—*satori*. That is the Zen word for enlightenment. In a flash Tenko was utterly convinced that the Absolute One—"call that one God, or Buddha, Brahman, Allah, or whatever"—was loving and giving, like that mother. In that instant in 1905, 33-year-old Tenko realized that the Absolute One was real, truly loved Tenko and every creature, and passionately desired to nourish, console, and sustain them. If you read the history of Zen in Japan you will often come upon cases of instantaneous, exhilarating, energizing, life-changing *satori*, like Tenko's. The latter took his joyful conviction to the people of Kyoto and beyond, helping thousands upon thousands find meaning and peace of heart through his writings, lectures, and the schools he built. His *Itto-En*, the religious movement he founded, spread throughout Japan and to Hawaii and California. One of its main tenents was "serving others with love and joy." In 1947 he was elected to the Diet (the Japanese parliament).

Tenko, in refusing to name the Absolute One "God or Buddha, Brahman, or Allah," was alluding to something the great Christian philosopher and Bible commentator of the thirteenth-century, St Thomas Aquinas, pointed out sharply. God is so utterly beyond the grasp of the puny human mind that what we know about him is far less than what we do not know. A great Australian disciple of Aquinas, the philosopher Fr. Austin ("Doc") Woodbury, SM, was brought up on the Hawkesbury River in New South Wales where, as a youth, he developed a passionate love of cattle-breeding, cricket, and down-to-earth thinking and expression. "Doc" summed up in typical Woodbury-ese what the medieval master Thomas had said:

We only know God like–y, not–y and more–y. We know he is *like* the beautiful, ordered universe he made—he is mirrored for instance in the wildly lovely Hawkesbury country. God is *not* like the limitations found in all his creatures, such as weakness, tiredness, and mortality. And we know that he is infinitely *more* than you, me, and all other creatures that he created in time.

Many of the great Greek philosophers understood and taught this. They felt sadness at not being able to know the Unmoved Mover more intimately. Biblical revelation, of course, offers a positive response to that sadness—for those who earnestly and prayerfully "seek" God. The expression "those who *seek* him," or its equivalent, occurs 165 times in the Old Testament! Open the psalms and you quickly find the expression. For instances; start with Psalms 9:11; 14:2; 22:27; 24:6; 27:8; 34:11; 40:17; 53:3; and so on.

Dedicated experts like Stuhlmueller and Bernhard Anderson have spent their adult lifetimes "seeking" the deep truths the Holy Spirit has put into so many psalms, psalms that might strike you at first sight as ordinary. One of their tools for mining this rich ore is knowledge of the original Hebrew and Aramaic words. One such word is *rahamin*, and it has become pure gold for me, thanks to Carroll Stuhlmueller. The word comes from *rehem*, meaning womb. *Rahamin* is the feeling a mother has for the child of her womb—a child still in her womb or already born from her womb. This word, found in dozens of psalms, has no single equivalent word in English and is rendered in various ways in the Bibles we use, such as "pity," "mercy," and "compassion." The *New American Bible* and the *Jerusalem Bible* are much closer to the original Hebrew with their translation "tenderness."

Inspiration that was both powerfully comforting and strengthening flooded into our hearts as we sat listening to

Stuhlmueller, his eyes shining and face aglow. His love of the psalms was infectious, which is why his classes, whether at the Chicago C.T.U. or the Tokyo Summer Schools, were packed. He gave us an invaluable tip on how to make the psalms our familiar friends and guides on the journey Home: Remember they are poems, written from and for the "heart"—what chapter 2 of Paul's first letter to the Corinthians called the "spirit," which is our deepest and truest knowing faculty. Our minds are very useful, but minds alone cannot create great marriages or happy families, nor peace of heart and a true love of God, nor great symphonies such as Beethoven's "Eroica," nor the deepest knowledge of the Scriptures. These are of the spirit—above all of the Spirit speaking to human spirits, human hearts. The Holy Spirit spoke to the hearts of the psalmists and they have recorded what he said in that language of the heart called poetry. Cardinal Newman's heraldic motto captured this: *Cor ad cor loquitor*, Heart speaks to heart.

Poetry is not always understandable at first reading. Take the classic yet sad example of the Jesuit Gerard Manly Hopkins. Today he is acknowledged as one of the greats of English verse—but he was dead twenty-nine years before anyone thought the manuscripts of his poems were worth publishing! His "The Wreck of the Deutschland" stirs people today with its sheer grandeur, power, and symbolism. In the small hours of December 6, 1875—hours made desperately darker by a heavy snowstorm driven before wild winds—a German ship, the *Deutschland*, went off course onto a sandbank in the Thames estuary. The vessel stuck fast, at the mercy of the waves and the snow. Sixty were drowned before help arrived thirty hours after the accident. One of the victims was a six foot tall Franciscan nun, who kept calling above the gale: "O Christ, come quickly." Hopkins submitted his poem to the Jesuit Henry Coleridge, editor of the prestigious English magazine *The Month*. The editor vaguely but firmly declined publishing the poem. The priceless manuscript would gather dust in a drawer for thirty-two years before anyone recognized its greatness; the psalms meet a similar fate in many an unthumbed Bible.

J. R. R. Tolkien wrote books loved the world over by children and adults, office workers and professors. His 500,000-word epic, *The Lord of the Rings*, sold 250,000 copies in the United States of America the first year it appeared. Tolkien's books, which are essentially parables of the continuing warfare between ultimate good and ultimate evil, are full of deeply poetic symbolism, easy to miss at a first, cursory reading. Tolkien's first book, *The Hobbit*, was read by an unimpressed publisher's reader and dumped into a reject drawer! The publisher's adult son was cleaning out the drawer, found it, saw its worth, and made a mint for the firm! We all can make a personal mint if we take the time to understand the historical background of the psalms and, with the help of great scholars like Stuhlmueller, get in touch with the encouraging and uplifting insights that the psalmists often expressed through poetic symbol and metaphor.

That the Holy Spirit should inspire psalm after psalm to tell us that the Father loves us with *rahamin*, sent shivers of emotion through Stuhlmueller, and we in his class began to share them. Very few of us had a mother who rejected us. Even if we did, Isaiah 49:15 assures that the child of God's womb will always be "cherished" ("receive *rahamin*"). Psalm 27:10 says the same. The books of Isaiah and Jeremiah deeply influenced the psalms, which developed by being added to and subtracted from throughout Israel's tempestuous history. We have seen how the invasion and captivity by Babylon made the redactors of the psalms rethink Israel's earlier self-confident enthusiasm for the Davidic kings.

Another book with a great influence on many of the psalms is Zephaniah, written around 630 BC, around forty years before Babylon's invasion. In a time of moral depravity and religious confusion not unlike our own, Zephaniah prophesied a national collapse. However he wrote that under God a "remnant" of faithful Israelites would keep the true faith. Zephaniah 2:3 and 3:12 say that these will be *anawim* (*ani* in the singular). After the Babylonian tragedy this word will appear sixty-nine times in the psalms. The *ani* was the one without wealth or power, and therefore often despised and victimized, yet at peace within because of his or her great trust in YHWH. The *ani* sang the psalms and rejoiced in the frequently occurring word *rahamin*. No matter how poor they might be in material goods and socio-political influence they were royalty, they were children of the very womb of God! YHWH was their very own kin! The old person who redacted that little gem Psalm 131—Stulmueller believed that the Hebrew words and grammar indicated someone looking back over a long lifetime—passes the final years "as a contented infant in its mother's arms." A spiritual second childhood, to use Paul Ricoeur's telling phrase.

For the Christian, these psalms that present the believer as kin, as a very child of YHWH, prepare for the time of great fulfillment when a young woman in that hick village Nazareth was chosen and overshadowed by the Holy Spirit. Because she said "Yes" our mothers and fathers could take their children to a crib at Christmas time, and tell us to kneel lovingly because the child Jesus is our God and our eldest brother. I once heard a tape recording of a Mass in Dublin, where the preacher said: "To be sure, we are all relatives of Jesus, on his mother's side." St Francis of Assisi made the first crib, and we are told he placed a peasant's newly-born child in the straw manger. He told the first Franciscans that when they built a church they must always have an image of Mary close to the sanctuary.

Il Poverello, which is almost Italian for the Hebrew *ani*, knew how much Christ's mother had helped him to understand that the Son of God had really become his brother. A modern songwriter calls Mary "our little sister who carried the Sun." She, Christ's most faithful disciple, teaches us the motherly tenderness of our Father in heaven.

If you read Pope John Paul II's powerful encyclical "On the Mercy of God" (*Dives in misericordia*), published in Advent 1980, you will find a moving description of God's *rahamin*, his "mother love," in section 9. In the previous section, the Pope discusses the more masculine *hesed*-love of God for his covenant people.

We have three millennia of strong souls telling us to "taste and see how good is the Lord" (Ps 34:9). That is the way, the Holy Spirit's way, for us to use the psalms. That requires prayer, requires what Mary does in Luke's Gospel—"treasuring these things in her heart." You might be interested in some *rahamin* texts to taste, to treasure in prayer:

> Have mercy on me, O God in your goodness [*hesed*], in your compassion [*rahamin*], cleanse me of sins (Ps 51:1). O Lord . . . always merciful and tenderhearted [*rahamin* in adjective form] (Ps 86:15). . . . Crowning you with love [*hesed*] and tenderness [*rahamin*], . . . YHWH is . . . tender [*rahamin*] . . . and loving [*hesed*] (Ps 103:4,8). YHWH is merciful, tenderhearted [*rahamin* in adjective form] . . . and very loving [*hesed*] (Ps 145:8).

Exodus 34:6 is a seminal experience for Moses. YHWH appears to him and says of himself: "YHWH, YHWH, a God of tenderness [*rahamin*] . . . and rich in love [*hesed*]."

8 Rahamin Continued— Waiting in the Darkness

STUHLMUELLER WOULD BECOME VISIBLY MOVED AS HE developed the implications of *rahamin* for us spellbound students: we are unconditionally loved as children of the womb of the God who is a tender-hearted Mother—as well as the dynamic Father-Creator of every part of being and beauty in the cosmos. Stuhlmueller had the heart of a poet in tune with the optimistic poetry of the psalms, but he was very much a realist aware of the pain and darkness in the human realm.

Several nights a week Stuhlmueller went swimming in a pool quite a few blocks distant from C.T.U., to ease a bad back problem. I went with him often to this pool, which was situated in a predominantly black area. He told me there was no longer any pool segregation in the United States but that we would be the only whites seen there. Every one of the black Americans we saw in the pool, he added, would almost certainly carry emotional wounds from insults or worse that "Whitey" had given him since childhood. Stuhlmueller went to this pool in the hope of easing some of this pain by his friendliness. He told me this with pain showing in his eyes. Quite a few times he grieved aloud about the violence and compromise in the America he loved—and in the Church he loved. He was obviously pained by the wrangling, bitterness, accusation, and counter-accusation among people arguing about "our God of peace"!

Commenting on Psalm 63's "soul pining for God like a parched weary land in a time of drought," Stuhlmueller touched on the unnerving sights you see in the growing number of old people's homes. He had just been on a poignant visit to his old teacher and friend, Barnabas Ahern, once a Bible scholar of world renown and the trusted peritus to the U.S. bishops at the Second Vatican Council. Alzheimer's disease had now reduced Ahern to a jibbering zombie. Stuhlmueller commented that a number of us in that classroom would almost certainly have to traverse that weird twilight existence in the last stages of our journey. He continued:

> Only a realistic prayer life, such as the psalms teach, will prevent us losing our nerve at this frightening prospect. The psalms often concentrate painfully on present suffering and future threats, but all (except Psalm 39 and the gloomiest, Psalm 88) end with at least quiet confidence because YHWH is always close by the faithful believer.

God told Moses in Exodus 3:14 that he was YHWH, a mysterious and archaic Hebrew form of the verb "to be" that Stuhlmueller translated as "I am he who will always be there".

From the quiver in his voice that day it seemed obvious that Stuhlmueller had taken his fears to YHWH in prayer, following his visit to Ahern, now in the shadows of a mental no-man's land. It also seems obvious that Stuhlmueller said "Yes Lord, if that is what you choose for me, too." Because YHWH would be there, Stuhlmueller could face with tranquility the possibility of slipping off the edge of conscious existence, into the black hole of Alzheimer's. On February 12, 1994, a massive stroke felled Stuhlmueller like the Lebanon cedar brought crashing down by that Mediterranean storm in Psalm 29. They rushed him unconscious to intensive care. His Passionist provincial opened the envelope containing Stuhlmueller's will and read that no extraordinary life-support systems were to be used, except those "which a non-industrialized country can offer its citizens." Stuhlmueller had long found peace in the company of the *anawim*, the poor of YHWH. The provincial asked the doctors whether there was the slightest chance of survival. They shook their heads, so the provincial consulted Stuhlmueller's family, and then had him unhooked from the medical equipment. They transferred the slumped genius to his small cell in the Chicago monastery. There followed an extraordinary outpouring of weeping visitors, prayer meetings, telephone calls, letters, faxes, and messages from all over the United States, Israel, and the rest of the world. Passionist friends contacted many of us ex-students, asking for prayers. Carroll Stuhlmueller was a great soul-friend who had taught us to meet the Lord and ourselves in the psalms. When I was phoned the sad news from Japan by a weeping Passionist priest, my mind went back to Stuhlmueller's second teaching about *rahamin*.

Rahamin assures us of the absolute kinship-love, blood-love, mother-love that God has for us. But it also reminds us that we often have to wait helpless in the darkness as a mere embryo of what God intends us to be. Stuhlmueller would draw on the many places in Scripture where the Holy Spirit uses this metaphor. In Genesis 1:1–2 our cosmos, the ground of our physical being, is *tohu we bohu*, which the *Jerusalem Bible* translators tell us means "trackless waste and emptiness." We are further told "there was darkness over this watery mass." That is the lightless womb of all human history—marvellously symbolized by the nine months each of us spent in the watery darkness of our mother's womb, with eyes and faculties that we could not use, totally helpless and dependant on our mothers. And then we read the beautiful: "God's Spirit hovered over the waters." The *Jerusalem Bible* has a footnote explaining "hovered": it is like the bird in Deuteronomy 32:11, "an eagle watching its nest, hovering over its eaglet, spreading out wings to hold it, supporting it on its pinions." The Hebrew word for "spirit" is *ruah*, which is feminine in that language. The (coldly?) philosophical Greek word for spirit is *pneuma*, which is without gender! The pragmatic (macho?) Romans called it *spiritus*, which is masculine in gender! The ancient Syrian Church, using a form of Aramaic close to the feminine Hebrew, spoke of "our mother, the Holy Spirit."

The word "womb" comes often into Scripture. In Psalm 22 the psalmist, describing a terrifying dark night of the soul, stops to remember in verses 9–10 that the Lord "took me from the womb . . . from my mother's womb you have been my God." The crucified Jesus quoted Psalm 22:1, "My God, my God, why have you forsaken me?" as he hung suspended in that terrible black hole of the spiritual cosmos. I wish I could find the name of the French poet, quoted by Dr Nagai of Nagasaki, who said the hole dug in Calvary to hold up the Cross became "the navel of the world." The People of God were sustained by the psalms through dark-as-the-womb situations like the Babylonian captivity and the still more brutal Roman occupation. They sang them in the synagogue, around the kitchen table, or over a child who did not want to go to sleep. The exquisite Psalm 131 was surely used this latter way by many a Jewish mother and father. The psalms were the people's prayer book. They were and are not the preserve of scholars who sometimes take more delight in seeking semantic oddities and even philosophical inconsistencies than in "seeking his face." The early Christians knew little if anything of "higher biblical criticism," nor knew those daunting German words that not a few modern Bible commentators bandy about smugly, as if to say: Now with these keys we can at last unlock the Scriptures! But those early Christians, seeking YHWH while reading, praying, and singing the psalms, discovered "the treasure hidden in the field." They kept the faith through the Roman persecutions and handed it on to us. If you read those early Christian writers fittingly called "the Fathers", men such as Irenaeus, Justin, Cyprian, Origen, Cyril, the two Gregories, Ephrem, Ambrose, and Augustine, it is obvious that the psalms fired their hearts. They loved these poems of the Holy Spirit, who hid a hundred hints of the Father's tender love and of his wise directions on how to find peace and our way Home. The spirit would most willingly aid honest "seekers." But, not all that easily!

The Spirit God is portrayed as a gentle dove, but also as a parent eagle in Deuteronomy 32:11 and Exodus 19:4. He is *El Shaddai*, "the Mountain God," the Eagle God who wants us to strengthen our wings, to risk buffeting mountain winds, seeking the freedom and the vision of high mountains. Scripture tells us a number of times that YHWH's "eagles" often sought the safety of becoming domestic hens, or "chooks", to use the expressive Australian slang word. Chooks have wings but don't risk flying, preferring to spend their day with eyes glued to the muddy ground looking for scraps. Any rotten scraps will do. They are birds gone wrong—they have no pride, go hysterical when approached with a bucket of slops, and shove and fight one another in a mad rush to gobble it all down, often trampling the scraps into the mud in the process. They are like our spiritual ancestors liberated by Moses, who complained there was no garlic, leeks, or meat in the desert, pining for fuller bellies and permanent shelter under slavemaster Egyptians! Psalms like 78:8 and 95:10 express YHWH's grief at seeing his eagle people opt for the worm's-eye vision of chooks.

Stuhlmueller, as befitted a man who joined a religious order dedicated to preaching about Jesus' Passion as the prelude of the Resurrection, often invited his students to discover in times of darkness invitations to die to old ways that had grown tired and constricting. Risking a re-entry into God—our Mother's Womb, as it were—we can be led to new births. The Lord leads us to fulfill new potentialities if we have the faith and courage to wait in the darkness. This demands the humbling experience of feeling helpless like a child in the womb again. Stuhlmueller asked us to reflect on the cries of the Terrible Psalms like Psalms 22 and 88, and to remember that roughly a third of the 150 psalms are laments about often gut-wrenching pain. Psalm 22's "O God, why have you abandoned me?" is a cry of desperation. There is near-despair also in Psalm 88:15–18: "Wretched, slowly dying since my youth, I bore your terrors. I am exhausted . . . You have destroyed me . . . You have turned my friends and neighbors into enemies. The one companion I have left is darkness."

9 *The Waters of Chaos*

THE BIBLE IS NOT A SCIENCE PRIMER NOR A HISTORY TEXT, BUT a "salvation history" storybook. Vatican II's Constitution on Divine Revelation, chapter 3, sums this up for Catholics: ". . . the books of Scripture must be acknowledged as teaching firmly, faithfully, and without error that truth which God wanted put into the sacred writings for the sake of our salvation." That is the infallible core of the Bible, the teachings that lead us on a sure if sometimes difficult road that will eventually get us to heaven. The Holy Spirit did not inspire the Bible to satisfy human curiosity about matters like the beginning and future of the visible universe, the validity of the Big Bang theory or Einstein's ideas on relativity, or how to make cool millions.

The Holy Spirit's journeymen who wrote the Scriptures were flesh and blood people who taught his salvation truths by employing the parlance, concepts, and idioms of their day—even if these do not stand up to the findings of modern telescopes and Carbon-14 dating. The sun "rose," the universe was created "in six days," etc. Sometimes you have to study ancient history and mythology to understand the terminology and message of the psalms (and other books of the Old Testament). Archaeologists can be a great help. Bible scholars like Bernhard Anderson and A. A. Anderson, aided by archaeologists and experts in ancient languages, give many of the psalms a new vividness and dynamism by explaining, for instance, the mythical "Waters of Chaos" that are so often referred to. For years I read the Psalms in total ignorance of this mythical metaphor, to my own loss.

Genesis 1:1–2, like many psalms, teaches the first salvation-history truth—that YHWH created the universe and everything in it—by employing the epic and picturesque cosmology accepted generally by ancient Israel and her neighbors in Canaan, Syria, Assyria, and Mesopotamia. The Hebrew words in Genesis 1:1–2 for the first stages of the creation of the cosmos are *tohu* (trackless waste), *bohu* (a great expanse of emptiness), and *tehom* (a watery abyss). Over all of this, God's Spirit "hovers" (the same word the Bible uses later for God as an eagle "hovering over its young in the nest," (Deut. 32:11). In Genesis 1:6, God creates a dome, a ceiling in the sky to prevent the vast waters of the abyss above from crashing down on the earth below. Rain falls (according to the cosmology that Israel and her neighbors accepted) when God opened sluices in the sky ceiling. The earth was anchored precariously on the waters of a vast ocean below it. These waters above, below, and around the earth were filled with mystery and terror for the ancients, who described them as the Waters of Chaos. They were only held back from overwhelming the earth, as they almost did in Noah's time, by YHWH, who alone could control them. Chesterton loved the world of ancient myth that taught so many great truths. His poem "The Wild Knight" speaks of God as "Conqueror of Chaos in a six days' war, With all the sons of God shouting for joy . . ."

In the creation myths of Israel's neighbors, there is always a battle between a good god like Baal or Marduk, and the evil thing dwelling in the Waters of Chaos. Timiat the "primeval Deep," Leviathan the sea monster, or Yam (Sea) or Nahar (River), are names for this hideous thing. We can understand the use or the name Nahar (River) in the lands where the rivers Tigris and Euphrates could suddenly turn into raging flood waters. Chaotic waters are the abode of evil gods and the Bible often refers to them in the continual battle between God and Chaos. Job 3:8 and 40:25 speaks of Leviathan, and Isaiah 27:1 of "Leviathan, the fleeing, twisting serpent." Isaiah 51:9–10 uses idioms from the Marduk-verses-Timiat myth: "Did you not split Rahab [or Timiat] in two, running that dragon through? Did you not dry up . . . the waters of the Great Abyss?" Psalm 74:14 speaks of how God "crushed Leviathan's heads . . . opening the spring, the torrent, drying up inexhaustible rivers." YHWH, unlike the gods Marduk and Baal, is not in mortal fear of the evil gods of chaos like Leviathan, Timiat, Yam, and Nahar. Psalm 104:26 tells us that Leviathan is YHWH's "plaything."

YHWH is always utterly more powerful than the evil force(s) of chaos, but the latter never cease raging against YHWH's goodness. Scripture often draws on the myth of epic battle to warn us of the mortal dangers we must face and to call us to ally ourselves with YHWH in the fight with chaos (sin, selfishness, hatred, alienation, bitterness, immorality, etc. Compare Paul's words on the deeds of the "flesh" in Galations 5:19–21, as opposed to the "fruits of the Spirit.") Ezechiel 29:3 reads: "The Lord YHWH says this: Now I set myself against you. Pharaoh, King of Egypt, you great *tannin* [meaning sea monster or crocodile] wallowing in your Nile." Evil tyrants like Pharaoh become contemporary Leviathans and Timiats.

Psalm after psalm draws on the then-current idiom of the Waters of Chaos, and sometimes on the sea monsters, in describing the ongoing battle between God and evil. Psalm 74:13–14 reads: ". . . You split the sea in two and crushed the heads of the dragons of the waters. You smashed Leviathan's heads making him food for dolphins." A. A. Anderson comments: "The appropriation of foreign myths and their re-interpretation by the Israelites was not a sign of weakness but rather an expression of their theo-logical vitality." Chesterton said that some mighty truths are contained in great non-biblical myths. He borrowed dragons and the like from them in his own epic poems, knowing that poetry can communicate some truths better than prose, especially the deeper truths of the Spirit.

Many of the psalms employ poetic expressions and metaphors from the great Middle Eastern myths, among which the Waters of Chaos is very common. Take Psalm 18:5–12, for instance. The psalmist calls the deadly perils threatening him "the *waters* of death and the *torrents* of Belial" (a god of death in the ancient Near East, and a name for Satan in the New Testament). Verse 7 has YHWH the Warrior God come into the battle, like valiant Baal and Marduk, the mythical warrior gods who fought chaos. YHWH is accompanied by mythical earthquakes and lightning flashes as he was when he came to the Israelites at Mt Sinai. YHWH's intervention to help the psalmist in dangers here and now is essentially the same as his help to Moses' Israelites. The psalm uses extravagant symbols to startle the reader into realizing the huge issues at stake. The colossal liberator of Exodus, YHWH, will deliver me from my present perils if I call upon him. Of course his victory and my full deliverance might take "forty years"! YHWH rides on the wind (v. 10), thunders from heaven (v. 13) and lets fly with arrows, scattering his foes (v. 14). These are expressions straight form the Canaanite myth of the warrior god Baal defeating evil that is named Yam (wild sea god) or Nahar (turbulent river god), or Mot (god of death). Stuhlmueller was deeply moved that the Holy Spirit would employ the very words of the ancient Canaanite myth that "attempts primarily to communicate an awesome, even terrifying sense of the momentous battle of goodness and evil, of God and demons, being waged within the events of history" (Stuhlmueller, *Psalms 1*, p. 130).

Catholic missionaries in China, India, and Japan could hardly be called highly successful! Why? I think the majority, with noble exceptions like Vilignano (Japan), Ricci (China), and de Nobili (India) traveled on the coat-tails of colonialism. The colonial masters looked down on the "natives" and missionaries followed suit, theologically and spiritually. By the time of Vatican II missionaries had seen the light, and gave witness to their personal experience of grace at work among non-Christians. Vatican II's teaching on other religions changed Catholicism forever. This is reflected in the subsequent official gatherings of Asian bishops. They issued key theological and pastoral documents at Taipei (1974), Baguio, Philippines (1978), Calcutta (1978), and Tokyo (1979). Referring to the non-Christian religions of their ancestors, the Asian bishops at Taipei in 1974 recognized in them "significant and positive elements in . . . God's design of salvation . . . from which contemporaries do not cease to draw light and strength." The Calcutta meeting called on Asian Christians to join non-Christians in dialogue "and prayer that will teach us what we can receive from them, what the Holy Spirit has taught others to express in their religious books in a marvellous variety of ways . . . through which we too may hear his voice, calling us to lift up our voices to the Father." The bishops insisted on a dialogue based on prayer because the Bible is not philosophy, just as Paul told the Corinthians, Greeks who were probably understandably tempted to a certain national pride in their philosophical abilities. The Bible is revelation, which, as Pascal said, is received on one's knees.

Many of you would have read the Indian Jesuit Anthony de Mello's books with pleasure. He gave several powerful retreats on prayer in Japan in which he humorously but trenchantly criticized post-Reformation Catholicism's over-reliance on rational efficiency. Some of his statements include: "Lose your minds and come to your senses . . . In prayer don't make resolutions, make petitions." He lamented later generations of his fellow Jesuits changing the "contemplation" of the founder Ignatius into "mental prayer." De Mello, who followed Jesus' method of telling stories, quoted much about the heart from Buddhist and Hindu sources. Summing up de Mello said: "The head is a very good place for prayer to begin but a very poor place for it to end up." Ditto for theology, ditto for Bible reading. De Mello thought priests and religious were wasting their own and others' time if they weren't good at praying.

As a Passionist seminarian, Stuhlmueller was taught by Barnabas Ahern, one of the pioneers of the contemporary biblical movement that recalled Catholicism to its roots in the Scriptures (and the early "Fathers"). Ahern passed on to Stuhlmueller his own belief in and love for the Scriptures. Stuhlmueller was sent to Rome, gaining a licentiate *cum laude* at the Pontifical Bible Institute in 1954. He returned to the United States, teaching Scripture and writing in biblical journals. When Cardinal Meyer of Chicago took Ahern to Rome as his Scripture *peritus* for Vatican II, Stuhlmueller took over Ahern's work for the *Jerome Biblical Commentary*.

Stuhlmueller spent the rest of his life, personal and professional, focused on the Bible. In 1966 he went back to Rome, gaining a doctorate from the Pontifical Biblical Commission, which is notoriously difficult to obtain. By the time he died in 1994, Stuhlmueller had been president of the U.S. Catholic Biblical Association and the Chicago Society of Biblical Research, general editor of prestigious *The Bible Today*, and on the editorial board of *The Journal of Biblical Studies* and *Catholic Biblical Quarterly*. He founded Chicago Catholic Theological Union's Israel Study Program, which has sent over 1000 students from around the world to study in the Holy Land. He wrote scores of influential articles and twenty-three books on the Bible.

I've met people from all over the world who every day

use his biblical meditations for daily Mass readings. I have a close friend from the North Coast of New South Wales, Australia, a highly successful businessman, owner of the city's newspaper and radio station, and so active in charity work that he has a Retirement Village called after him. He travels a lot, and although he might sometimes forget his comb, he never forgets Stuhlmueller's biblical meditations—plus his bulky *Jerusalem Bible* to look up the Scripture references! That was Stuhlmueller—he gets you seeing and loving the Word of God as the surest, gentlest, and strongest guide to living.

On his 65th birthday, leading Bible scholars in the United States, including a Rabbi, brought out a Festschrift, a collection of essays on Stuhlmueller's work. It was entitled, very perceptively, *Scripture and Prayer*.

But back to Psalm 18. Verses 15–18 describe a struggle of cosmic proportions. "At the blast of the gale of his wrath the sea beds are laid open, the foundations of the earth left exposed." The psalmist is part of these fearful upheavals: he is caught up "in the deep waters," struggling with "a powerful enemy, with foes too strong for me." Only YHWH can master them and save him. This furious battle with evil and superhuman forces that will destroy us, unless YHWH the warrior comes to help us, is highlighted in many psalms (Ps. 24:8, 35:1–3; Ps. 144:1–2, 7–8, etc.). Psalm 149:6 gives us some of the words of "the new song": we are YHWH's people who "praise him highly with their voices, while their hands hold two-edged swords." Jeremiah, who had such a deep influence on the psalms, sings to "YHWH at my side, the mighty warrior."

In 1995 we commemorated the 50th anniversary of the overthrow of incarnate evil, Hitler and his Nazi follows. One of the millions butchered by that evil was Lutheran paster Dietrich Bonhoeffer. He chose confrontation with Germany's totalitarian government when he could easily have accepted a prestigious job offer in the United States in 1939. He was imprisoned in 1943 and hanged on April 9, 1945. Disturbed by the soft option that many German Christians took, he warned them in *The Cost of Discipleship* that there is no such thing as "cheap grace" in the Bible. A great lover of the psalms, Bonhoeffer castigated believers who would choose only the "nice" ones, detouring around the "hard" ones. Faced by the evil faces of Nazism, he became very conscious that one essential teaching of the psalms is the ongoing struggle with temptation to compromise, selfishness, arrogance, using others, and soft living. You only become intimate with the God of love if you are prepared to seek him, and often struggle painfully in that seeking. This is the stuff of the Gospels, the Epistles, and, most clearly, the New Testament's last book, Revelation. Each of us must freely chose.

This uncompromising message has been reiterated in modern times at Lourdes and Fatima. Five million pilgrims go each year to Lourdes. Only a very small number of physical cures are witnessed but spiritual healings abound. Many find peace, meaning in suffering, and Gospel certitude. These two places seem to anger other people. Why? I suspect because Our Lady at Lourdes and Fatima clearly spoke of that terrible mystery that disturbs us all, the possibility of eternal alienation from God. Put bluntly, damnation! A chilling mystery hard to accept, which I and most priests dislike preaching about. How could a loving God allow eternal alienation? For that matter, how does a loving God allow little children to suffer leukemia, or worse, parents who abuse them sexually? It is a mystery. Many decide it is a cruel contradiction and opt for atheism.

To be a believer you must be prepared to live with mystery and with struggle. The Waters of Chaos psalms tell us that God is struggling with us. He told Moses "I am called YHWH," the archaic Hebrew verb form that Stuhlmueller translated: "I am he who will always be there."

10 The Waters of Chaos Continued

C. S. LEWIS, OXFORD LECTURER AND CAMBRIDGE PROFESSOR, relinquished atheism for the Christian faith in his early thirties. He accepted the Bible, *but* many of the psalms put him off! They made God seem like a proud millionaire demanding that his staff continually talk about his achievements! However Lewis gradually came to see that praising God doesn't add anything to him but gets us into the vibrant rhythm of reality and does our spirits good, just as nourishing food and vigorous exercise do our bodies good! About two and a half millennia earlier Isaiah 61:11 put it this way: "As the earth makes fresh things grow and a garden makes seeds blossom, the Lord YHWH makes . . . praise blossom in the sight of the Gentiles." It is as natural for us to praise the Creator as it is for the good earth to produce growing things. In 1958 Lewis published his masterful book *Reflections on the Psalms*. His lofty mind had come to respond to their epic, cosmic, and salvific dimensions. Lewis the writer loved to employ the literary genres of mythology and allegory as you will know if you've read his Narnia books, or *That Hideous Strength*. The latter is the last of his interplanetary trilogy describing the cosmic struggle between good and evil. Lewis admired and is sometimes likened to another English writer and convert to the faith, G. K. Chesterton, a poet very much at home with allegory and the great myths. Lewis said of

Chesterton's book-length (and surely greatest) poem, *The Ballad of the White Horse*, it "takes hold of you . . . shakes you and makes you want to cry . . . he achieves the heroic, the rarest quality in modern literature." The psalmists were poets who shake us, make us want to cry, and even cry out, shout, and clap, as the temple congregation did while chanting the psalms.

"Enthusiasm" comes from the Greek *en theos*, "in God." The psalmists were enthusiasts, as Jesus was ("I've come to cast fire on the earth, and how I long for the blazing," Lk. 12:49). Karl Rahner once said that cold, moralistic preachers create atheists! The psalmists had too much fire in their bellies to be accused of doing that, and it was fire that came from the Holy Spirit. That fire gave enough light to keep them from missing the way and wandering into the many false and destructive byways of non-revealed, mere mythic religions. There were the temple prostitutes of the Canaanites, for instance, or the burning alive of first-born male children to appease Moloch, a voracious god of the Ammonites. The fight against evil and chaos became all the more difficult when religious leaders encouraged evil acts and called them holy.

The Bible purified the myths. Psalm 29 is an adapted Canaanite hymn with clear resonances from the Waters of Chaos myth. It is a beautiful poem about a winter storm howling in from the Mediterranean, uprooting cedars on the Lebanon mountains and then veering south along the funnel of the River Jordan valley. The original Canaanite storm was both symbol and spawn of the terrible Waters of Chaos ("the waters, the multitudinous waters" of verse 3, and "the flood" of verse 10). But YHWH "sat enthroned above the flood," in his "palace" (his abode in heaven and on earth in the temple). His faithful can cry glory, not terror! They know YHWH is in control of the fearful waters. Because he created them he controls them. The psalm that began with destructive ferocity ends with "YHWH blesses his people with peace."

Psalm 42:7 reads: "Deep is calling to deep as your cataracts roar, all your breakers, your waves crash over me." The Hebrew word for "deep", *tehom*, is found in the cosmic myths of Israel's neighbors, and is also found in Genesis 1:2, where it is the deep that is covered in darkness. Psalm 42 is one of those titled "Of the Sons of Korah". If you read Numbers 16 you hear how their ancestor Korah, a priest and great-grandson of Levi the high priest, revolted against the authority of Moses. Korah and his descendants were demoted from a directly priestly role to menial service in the temple (as gatekeepers, breadbakers, etc.). There are twelve psalms titled "Of the Sons of Korah". Each has an element of lament or nostalgic pining for lost privileges. No one knows the precise trouble faced by the composer(s) of Psalm 42, but Stuhlmueller points out that these troubles, and the troubles of the readers who are meant to identify with the psalmist, are described in terms of *tehom*, the Waters of Chaos, with their fearful sea monsters like Tiamiat and Leviathan.

Jonah is hurled into the sea by terrified sailors, and says to YHWH: "You cast me into the abyss, into the midst of the sea, and the flood [*tehom*] enveloped me ... The waters surround me, up to my throat, the abyss was about me" (Jon 2:4–6). This mythic allegory runs through much of the Old Testament. It puts our personal struggles with evil, alienation, destruction, and temptation, into the realm of God's struggle to bring his kingdom of peace, goodness, and justice into human society.

Psalm 65:7–8 reads: "You settle the mountains in place by your strength, you who are girt with might. You quieten the clamour of the ocean and its waves, and the uproar of the nations." Stuhlmueller again sees clear reference here to the ancient cosmic chaos myth and concludes: "This links the people worshiping in the Jerusalem Temple with

God's world mission of forgiveness and new life for all peoples. The psalms teach a big and dynamic spirituality when you learn to read the allusions."

In Psalm 74, commentators point out clear references to the ancient cosmic myths, a "treasure-house of poetry on which poets and prophets liked to draw" (Eichrodt, quoted by A. A. Anderson in his commentary on this psalm). Psalm 74:12–14 reads: "Yet, God my king from of old, whose salvation deeds cover the earth, you split the sea with your power and crushed the heads of its dragons. You smashed Leviathan's heads, leaving it as feed for dolphins." Verses 18–23 appeal to God to smash the blaspheming despot who is a "Leviathan." With his soldiers he has invaded Israel, destroyed the temple, and pursued God's people even out into caves in the wilderness. Jews on the run from Nazis, and Christians in lands violently occupied and controlled by communist armies, understood this psalm! We ourselves, in a mad society that violently enters our living rooms and even little children's minds via godless and often mindless television, will identify with it if we are aware of what is happening beneath the gloss of the 1990s. We are meant to see ourselves and our times in the psalms as we pray them.

Psalm 77:16–17 employed the same cosmic myth. God proves too powerful for the waters (*tehom*) that in this psalm become the Red Sea. God splits it in two to allow Moses and the fleeing Israelites to escape Egypt. Verses 18–19 draw on metaphors from the then-current cosmic myths, as God continues to show his salvific dynamism in creating the covenant people at Mt Sinai—where his thunder and lightning "illumined the whole world" (v. 19). YHWH is greater than Baal. "Striding the sea," he shows himself greater than other gods, for God subdues the chaotic forces completely, whereas Baal and Marduk's struggle with them has no ending, no final conclusion. It was a treadmill fight against Mot (death, occurring every winter and re-enacted in temples, often accompanied by lewd rites with prostitutes or royal concubines.)

One who truly understands the psalms, says Stuhlmueller, sees that YHWH, the author of "past salvation deeds" that liberated his people, wants to enter into the contemporary struggles of his people. Psalm 89, first recited when a new Davidic king was crowned in Jerusalem, assures king and people that YHWH will be there with them, ever faithful to the covenant and all-powerful against the forces of evil and chaos. King and people must of course fulfill their side of the covenant. Again, the language of ancient myths is used. Archaeologist find in verses 5–6 actual phrases from an Assyrian hymn to Sin, the Nineveh Moon god, but now purified by monotheism. Verses 9–10 employ monsters from the old cosmic myth. YHWH splits Rahab in two. The mythical monster Rahab is another name for Leviathan, Timiat, and the Dragon, and personified the watery chaos. (It also sometimes means Egypt, of Ps. 87:4.) YHWH, who defeated primeval chaos and created the orderly, fruitful "good earth," was beside Moses when he defeated the evil pharaoh and is with the Jerusalem king and his people when they are fighting for God's law and covenant. When we recite the psalm today it assures us: YHWH is there with us in our personal struggles to keep his law and covenant. A.A. Anderson comments on Psalm 89:9: "The Israelites believed the world was continually threatened by chaos, and only by the might of YHWH were the destructive waters held back." We can say the very same today in our struggles to be authentic Christians. Evil is ever a threat, above all the evil that comes from within, as Jesus warned in Mark 7:21–22, enumerating "fornication, theft, murder, adultery, avarice, malice, deceit, indecency, envy, slander, pride, folly."

Of Psalm 104 Bernhard Anderson writes: "It has long been recognized that this psalm, both in form and content, is related to the beautiful Egyptian *Hymn to Aton*, found in the tomb of Pharaoh Akh-en-Aton (about 1380–1362 BC)" (*Out of the Depths* p. 28). This historical period is well before any psalms were written or even thought of, pre-dating even "the Sweet Singer of Israel," King David, by four centuries. Anderson adds that borrowed hymns like Psalms 104 and 29 "were transformed . . . and converted." The Holy Spirit inspired psalmists to make their composi-tions come alive for their contemporaries by borrowing from the prevailing pagan poetry with a marvelous free-dom that never, however, compromised the true faith. Psalm 104:7 borrows a common Middle Eastern myth and has YHWH and not Aton (often spelt Aten) putting the Waters of Chaos to flight. In verse 9 YHWH imposes lim-its on the waters' extension and power. Verses 10–11 see the terrible waters tamed by YHWH into springs that serve even lowly wild donkeys. Verses 13–14 show how useful and fruitful the once hell-bent-on-destruction waters have become, under YHWH's providence. This sec-tion is like a vocalization of Beethoven's Pastoral Symphony—after the wild storm harmony is restored and the countryside glistens as the sun shines resplendently through air washed clean.

Psalm 104:25–26 is quite a climax: "Then there is the sea, a vast expanse, teeming with life too multitudinous to be numbered, fish great and small. Ships pass back and forth, sailing above Leviathan whom you made as your plaything." Leviathan (and Timiat, the Dragon, the Fleeing Serpent, Rahab, and their equivalents) has lost its terror because the psalmist knows that YHWH not only subdues the Thing, he actually created it for his own pur-poses. In that beautiful "Psalm" of the three young men (Daniel 3:57–90), every part of creation is called to "bless the Lord and give glory and praise to him for his good-ness." In verse 60 "the waters above the heavens," once the dreaded Waters of Chaos, are told to bless YHWH.

Then follows a litany of forces of nature: winds, storms, animals tame and wild (including sea beasts!)—the terrifying elements in nature like lightening as well as the encouraging ones like gushing springs—all give glory to the Lord. That most joyful psalmist of thirteenth-century Assisi, St. Francis, wrote his own "Canticle of the Sun" in precisely this vein. Francis, like the three young men in Daniel, has met the Lord, has seen his face, and nothing is fearful anymore.

The depth psychologist Carl Jung pointed out that our very weaknesses, what he called our shadow side, can become strengths if we accept and befriend them. A terrible nightmare about me lying in a coffin might even be a wholesome message from the Holy Spirit, telling me to let die some dimension of my life that is now over—but to which I still cling. The wounds of Jesus became our opening into the Heart of God. St Francis rejoiced when he was granted the grace of bearing those wounds in his own body. The legend about how he tamed the killer wolf of Gubbio into becoming the friend of the villagers may or may not be historical, but the message is true, is biblical—God's Spirit continues to hover over the Waters of Chaos, bringing forth beauty and order, giving a purpose to every creature, even to Leviathan. The magnificent Alsatian dog that was once the wolf terrorizing German forests has become a faithful guardian of the home and gentle companion of little children.

Through "Remembering"— Exodus Now

For forty days Moses was learning to remember . . .
(St Irenaeus, *Against the Heresies*)

A GREAT POET IS A FREE SOUL NOT AFRAID OF BOLD NEW thinking "expressed in metaphors sparkling with the fires of the real" (Dr Austin Woodbury). There is great poetry in the psalms, composed by writers who learned boldness, freedom, and freshness of expression from the Holy Spirit. We have considered examples of this in the psalmists' use of the Waters of Chaos myth, of the Canaanite hymn to Baal the Storm god, and the Egyptian hymn to the supreme god Aton. The latter two became Psalms 29 and 104. Another extraordinary example of free composition is Psalm 105:33. Speaking of the plagues God sent against the Egyptian slave masters, the psalm says: "YHWH blasted their grapevines and fig trees." If you read the historical account in Exodus 9:23–31 YHWH's lightning and hail destroyed the Egyptians' "flax and barley." Flax and barley were indeed Egyptian crops, but to bring out what has been called the "Exodus Now" aspect, the psalm substituted crops that were grown by the Israelites who changed this account many generations later: grape vines and fig trees! There might even be a biblical fundamentalist who complains privately to the Holy Spirit that in doing this in the Scriptures, he is guilty of shifting the goal posts!

Stuhlmueller and most modern commentators on the psalms, point out that they grew mainly from and with the

Jerusalem temple liturgy. This liturgy was the reciting and remembering of the great salvific acts of God in Israel's history. Many of the people who participated faithfully in the liturgy ("seeking his face") had an extraordinary spiritual experience that kept them coming to the temple liturgy: what they remembered there began to happen here and now. For example, a worshiper might come to the temple service feeling quite broken. The spouse the person loves has walked out with a lover. Everything seems lost, hopeless, meaningless. But as the liturgy retells, for instance, the Exodus story, there comes a new peace with this profound realization—the God who saved the person's ancestors from slavery, despite an all-powerful pharaoh, his army, and the huge desert between Egypt and the Promised Land, is just as present and powerful, here and now, to help honest Israelites. Many Catholics attend daily Mass and in the same kind of faith hear the words: "Do this in remembrance of me." They do remember Jesus' love and his encouragement to the disciples at the Last Supper, as well as his promise to sacrifice himself for them. It begins to happen again at this Mass! I become the disciple whom Jesus loved and, if I am spiritually aware, I begin to desire to sacrifice this, my body and blood, my self and my own convenience for his Father's Kingdom and his people. If I am seeking to see his face at Mass, what happened on Holy Thursday and Good Friday begins to happen again now. Psalm 105:33's "grape vines and fig trees" in place of "flax and barley" is saying precisely that.

Exodus and Holy Thursday begin happening again when YHWH's people gather for authentic liturgical prayer. As a result Vatican II can make some extraordinary assertions in the Constitution on the Sacred Liturgy:

> . . . Christ is always present in his Church, especially in liturgical celebrations . . . it follows that every liturgical celebration, because it is an action of Christ the Priest and

of his Body, which is the Church, is a sacred action surpassing all others. No other action of the Church can match its efficacy . . . (section 7).

Stuhlmueller, in his commentary on Psalm 105, speaks of "this continuous Exodus celebrated and experienced." My Irish forebears knew nothing of Vatican II but they clung to the faith in the darkness of persecution and discrimination, and took the grave risk of liturgical worship (the Mass) in secret, out in the country on "Mass rocks" that are still pointed out to visitors. They experienced in their own lives what Vatican II would formally teach and a famous saying was born that Irish nuns handed on to me: "It is the Mass that matters." I've celebrated some funerals after tragic deaths and have had undertakers comment later in words like these: "I'm not of your faith but I've often noticed how Catholic funeral Masses can be so hopeful."

When little Bernadette was snatched from life by cot death, her parents Paul and Pauleen, and their families, were utterly devastated. The night before the funeral, I knelt with Paul and Pauleen in front of the statue of Mary in the Chapel of St Joseph's College, in Hunter's Hill, Sydney, Paul's old school. They sobbed out aloud to Mary, telling her they were trying to accept the good Father's will, as she had done in her darkness by the Cross. They placed their tiny Bernadette's soul in her loving arms, asking her to help them keep saying "Yes" to Jesus. The funeral was a spiritual love-songfest before a packed congregation. Paul was a leader of a popular music group and they and many other musicians sang the Mass. The parents were so magnificent that Caroline Jones heard about it and interviewed Paul on ABC radio for her acclaimed *Search for Meaning* program.

During that Requiem Mass I think most attending had a real experience of Christ and his mother present with us.

At the cemetery Paul took the tiny white coffin from the hearse and carried it to the grave, Pauleen beside him. In the darkness we saw the gentle light that comes from the bloodless body of the Crucified and the deathly pale face of the Valiant Woman standing beside him. What a multitude of broken people have seen that same light as they rejected despair, hatred, and self-pity at other desperately sad funerals. People have seen it too as they sought YHWH's help by reading Psalms 88, 44, or 131.

I noted earlier that Fr Raymond Tournay OP, an aging but agile professor at the famous *Ecole Biblique* in Jerusalem, has spent a lifetime studying the psalms. His monumental *Seeing and Hearing God with the Psalms* is literal proof of his extraordinary grasp of them. It that book he speaks of the quantum leap made by the broken Jews exiled to Babylon. Jerusalem, its temple, and the Davidic line had been destroyed in 587 BC, despite YHWH's apparent oaths that this would never happen! In Babylon they despondently gathered in small groups clinging to the one thing they had left, the memorized psalms. And then the miracle! They began to experience, in chanting these psalms the presence of YHWH, "to see his face," precisely as they had done in the temple. They obviously would have been allowed to carry few if any of the heavy Scripture parchments when they were force-marched to Babylon. But Stuhlmueller has said that if the whole Bible was destroyed except for the psalms you would still have a record of all the essential salvation history events!

The Jews' great discovery in Babylon was that by "remembering" God's past saving acts through reciting or chanting the psalms together, even in most un-templelike surroundings, they experienced those past salvation acts anew, and this gave meaning and hope to their lives in Babylon. This new way of "seeing his face" without the help of glorious temple rituals gave them courage to keep the faith and, in the persons of their children and grandchildren, to rebuild Jerusalem and the temple, and to reinstate those rituals with renewed devotion.

In 1976 I was working in the presbytery garden at Hunter's Hill, Sydney, when I was urgently called to Royal North Shore Hospital. Muriel and her husband Dick greeted me when I arrived. They had just received her X-rays and her doctor had told them the grim truth: "If I operate, Muriel, it will take away the pain but you will die before Christmas. If I do nothing there will be pain but you will live till February or so." Muriel had chosen the latter, and her husband had immediately phoned to ask me to come to the hospital and pray with them for peace of heart. I did that with sadness and when I left Muriel's room Dick accompanied me to the lift. There was a delay and we prayed quietly together on the deserted top floor, not noticing the nurse who came and stood behind us. In the lift she spoke to me: "Thank you. It's beautiful to see men not ashamed to pray in public." I told her of Muriel's bad news. Several days later I received a letter from Muriel:

> That lovely Protestant nurse dropped into my room late tonight. Finding me awake she told me of you and Dick praying while waiting for the lift. She gave me a piece of notepaper on which she had written: "Isaiah 43:1b–2. Do not be afraid because I have redeemed you. I have called you by your name, Muriel, you are mine. When you pass through the sea I will be with you and in rivers you will not drown. When you pass through fire you will not be burned, the flames will not kill you."

Muriel said she knew why the young nurse chose that text—cancer was a fire in her body and would destroy it, but she was sure it would not destroy her soul, the most real her. Her husband and family would be with her, praying and even celebrating a last Christmas with her, she wrote. I actually offered a Mass in her home that

Christmas, 1976. Muriel was bedridden and weak but bright eyed as her husband, their seven children and their own families poured out love and pride with the Mass prayers and hymns. We knew that Isaiah was being fulfilled, that YHWH was with Muriel, preventing the cancer from consuming her hopes, her faith, and her soul as she crossed that desert. It was Exodus Now!

There are dozens and dozens of places in the psalms where the Lord's salvific deeds are remembered in the liturgical assemblies. Psalm 111:1 says "I give thanks . . . where the people assemble. The works of the Lord . . . delight those who ponder them." Psalm 68:7 goes: "God, you set out at the head of your people and marched across the desert with them." Scholars tell us the Jews often had an actual procession during the chanting of such psalms, the levitical leaders reminding participants that YHWH was still with them on their journeys. Psalm 77:11 has: "Remembering YHWH's deeds, remembering his miracles in the past." Psalm 114 is a remembering of the heroic escape from Egypt across a hostile desert. The psalm is also a classic example of Stuhlmueller's reminder that the psalms are poetry. So "the sea fled," "the mountains skipped like rams, like lambs the hills. Sea, what makes you run away . . . Quake, earth at your master's coming . . ." The Israelites were in touch with the meaning of this poetry. They clapped, danced, and leapt along with it, helping the psalms to happen again, now.

The psalms kept the faith alive for the Jews in Babylon, and they will help us keep our faith during this present age when we live in a new kind of Babylonian captivity. The barbarians have broken down the city walls, are in our television sets with destructive philosophies of nihilism and relativism, with what's-the-use-ism, mindless violence, loveless sex, and with scorn for anyone who is certain that God is real, that Christian morality is authentic, or that Christ rose and is still with us.

12 YHWH "Who Is Making Us"

Psalms 95

AUSTIN (THE "DOC") WOODBURY WAS A MIGHTY TEACHER, enthusing his classes even when teaching an abstruse subject like metaphysics, or rather, especially teaching metaphysics, which is about ultimate realities and The Reality. He had fire in his belly, as they say, and fired great numbers of Sydneysiders—from medical professors to junior clerks—who attended his Aquinas Academy, just down from the Sydney Harbour Bridge. The Doc was passionate about truth and about God, convinced both could be discovered by people who really sought God. He loved the poetry of G.K. Chesterton, a thinker with the same convictions. The Doc would smile as he recited the conclusion of "The Convert," written when some freethinkers ridiculed Chesterton's reception into the faith in 1928, when he was 48 years old:

> The sages have a hundred maps to give
> That trace their crawling cosmos like a tree,
> They rattle reason out through man a sieve
> That stores the sand and lets the gold go free:
> And all these things are less than dust to me
> Because my name is Lazarus and I live.

In metaphysics both the Doc and Chesterton were vigorous optimists, finding great satisfaction in Genesis 1:31: "God saw all that he had made and indeed it was very good." The Doc had little patience with the philosophy of the freethinkers, and often remarked on their pessimism in the evening of their lives. H. G. Wells' open despair in his last book, *Mind at the End of its Tether*, was a case in point. The agnostic Swinburn also drew the Doc's ire. He called him "the poet of doubt, dirt, and despair." Swinburn's open anti-metaphysics led the poet to a stance against life, a kind of cult of death! Chesterton reacted with uncharacteristic anger against this rejection of the biblical cosmic optimism, and indeed of nature. One of his poems, "Ecclesiastes", begins:

> There is one sin: to call a green leaf grey,
> Whereat the sun in heaven shuddereth.
> There is one blasphemy: for death to pray
> for God alone knoweth the praise of death.

The Doc shared Chesterton's belief that truth is expressed in the good, plain words of ordinary people, and he encouraged his students to go back to the roots of words to better understand them. He would take a word like "companion," and point out its Latin roots, *com* (together) and *panis* (bread). The one you eat meals with usually becomes your friend, your companion. "Atonement" was "at-one ment," "ment" at the end of words meaning "that by which." He helped us understand important truths by going to the Latin, Greek, Anglo-Saxon, and other roots of the words used to express them. In doing so he also taught us to appreciate the craft of the wordsmith, and to value the intuitive common sense of our forebears—generally less educated than us but closer to nature—who fashioned so many words and sayings that got to the heart of reality.

Carroll Stuhlmueller did a similar thing, often taking considerable time to explain the Hebrew words used to express the Holy Spirit's original inspiration of the psalms (granting of course that no human words can capture this perfectly). In the Hebrew verb system, Stuhlmueller pointed out, time (past, present, future), is not the primary concern, but rather: Is the action complete or as yet incomplete? He gave us as an example Jeremiah 1:5: "Before I *formed* you in the womb (incomplete action verb) I *knew* you (complete action verb). Before you *came to birth* (incomplete action) I *consecrated* you (complete action)." God's knowing and consecrating Jeremiah for his task is a once and final action, perfectly complete. However God's forming of Jeremiah and Jeremiah's becoming the person God wants him to be is a process that will take all of Jeremiah's life on earth. A slow, progressive process! Stuhlmueller saw these incomplete action verbs, found in many psalms, as important and encouraging messages to anyone who recites the psalms "seeking his face."

You've probably heard of that vicious little bumper sticker, "I don't get angry, I get even!" There is another sticker that the ever-forgiving Stuhlmueller would have surely preferred: "Don't get mad at me—God hasn't finished yet!" Stuhlmueller had a great love for Psalm 95. Initially as a Passionist religious and then as a priest (ordained in 1950), he said this psalm each day as he began the Divine Office (or breviary). He would become excited about verse 6: "Let us prostrate ourselves, let us kneel before YHWH our Maker." In the original Hebrew it reads "YHWH who is making us." The incomplete, continuing action once again! YHWH is at work everywhere, and all the time, if we use the "eyes of our heart" to discern it. The religious authorities in Jerusalem tried to lay down conditions for how Jesus could work—definitely no healing of the sick on the Sabbath! Jesus refused, answering in John 5:17: "My Father goes on working and so do I!" I think St Augustine was trying to get his people to hear God's silent music all around them, and to discover the wonder of YHWH's dynamic "working" when he said: "God creates the universe new every morning!"

God is alive and wants us to be alive, fully alive. Amos 5:4 has him saying: "Seek me and you shall live." The third-century Rabbi Simlai said all the Bible's commandments can be reduced to that command! Stuhlmueller remarked that "those who seek him" is "a key expression and it occurs about 165 times in the Old Testament and frequently in the psalms." Stuhlmueller told me, somberly, that one dejected U.S. bishop asked him to come and speak to his priests about the psalms because "I've discovered that only 17 per cent of them recite the breviary!" The priest replied that if they were to energetically seek the treasure hidden in the field of the psalms, they would come to love the psalms so much, and gain so much encouragement and inspiration from then, that a team of horses couldn't keep them from praying the breviary daily. But, as with keeping a garden going or learning a computer program there is no way around intelligent, sustained effort! No miner ever made a living leaning on his shovel. We won't be able to mine the riches of the Holy Spirit hidden in the psalms unless we "seek," by study and prayer. Hard work, yes, but the returns are great.

A husband and wife take each other, and their marriage, for granted at their grave peril. A real marriage is an ever-ongoing affair. So is a biblical spiritual life. Jesus often spoke of the Kingdom of God, which in his Aramaic language is *Malkuth YHWH*, literally "where YHWH *is reigning*," remarked Stuhlmueller. Again, an ongoing, dynamic word! In Aramaic the name Jesus is similar, literally translated as "God is saving."

I'm writing this not far from Sydney, in a place called Toongabbie. Toongabbie, one of the first Aboriginal place-names used by Europeans in Australia, being first used officially in July 1792, means "Meeting of the Waters." When I came here in 1946 to study for the priesthood, an old Marist said to me: "In the spiritual life there is no marking time. If you're not going forward you're going backwards!

Never forget that." A little later I was somewhat shocked to read a kind of confirmation of Jesus' words in Revelation 3:15–17: "I know your deeds . . . neither hot nor cold . . . I wish you were one or the other . . . Because you are lukewarm . . . I will spit you out of my mouth . . . Little do you understand your wretched state." Stuhlmueller gave priests and religious a simple choice concerning the psalms: Study at least one of the good modern Scripture experts on the psalms, as you would study the latest automobiles if you wanted to make a living as a car salesman! Above all, give time to praying the psalms. Then you will "relish" them and you will be led ever forward by them. The other choice is to go on droning them because you have to (in the breviary or at Mass) and be bored to tears!

Let's take a quick look at Stuhlmueller's treatment of Psalm 95. He sees its origins as a procession hymn used when the congregation assembled at a place such as the Spring of Gihon in the deep valley below the Temple Mount in Jerusalem. The psalm was probably composed not long after the return from the exile in Babylon. As the congregation walked up the valley singing the psalm, they remembered the journey from Babylon as well as the desert journey from Egypt under Moses. Later, when belief in heaven became part of their faith, the Jews remembered they were on a journey of their own, here and now, from the oppression of worry, temptation, sickness, financial worries, etc., toward the perfect freedom of God's Promised Land. "Many journeys crisscross in this psalm," writes Stuhlmueller. They sang "acclaiming the rock of our salvation" (v. 1) as they gazed up to the huge rock of mountain to the northwest, on which stood the temple, the procession's destination. Passing the area where Solomon compromised his faith by building pagan temples to please his foreign wives who worshiped gods such as Baal, they sang repentantly: "YHWH is a great God,

greater . . . than all the gods" (v. 3). The next verse proclaims that YHWH made and controls "the sea," and
Stuhlmueller suggests the congregation would remember
how he won the fierce cosmic battle against the Waters of
Chaos. They probably carried libations of water from the
Gihon Spring to pour out in the temple, symbolizing
purification and maybe how YHWH changes the Waters
of Chaos, abode of killer monsters, to life-giving water. At
verse six the congregation would actually "kneel and
prostrate themselves" before "YHWH who is making us."
At Fatima, the three visionaries tell us the angel worshiped prostate before the chalice and host that appeared.
Moderns aren't too comfortable with prostrating, nor with
the grim parts of biblical revelation that Lourdes and
Fatima convey. But two millennia of great saints, such as
Anthony of the Desert in ancient times, Ignatius of Loyola
in the sixteenth century, and moderns like Fr Kolbe of
Auschwitz, found themselves in touch with the rhythm of
the real in prostrating themselves before the Lord, just like
our spiritual ancestors, the Jews.

Stuhlmueller thinks a short homily was preached at this
part of the psalm procession (as during the liturgical
chanting of many other psalms)—maybe some reflections
on the people who lost trust in God's providence as they
marched with Moses through the Sinai desert, some even
complaining there was no garlic!

Verse seven's "We are the people he pastures, the flock
he guides," again portrays a dynamic God ever at work to
lead true seekers to growth and freedom. The verse concludes: "If only you would listen to him today"—probably
a sentence from the homily. The frequent use of the word
"today" is a special feature of Deuteronomy, a book that
influenced many of the psalms profoundly. I've just read
Deuteronomy quickly and counted "today" thirty-two
times—and probably missed a few! For example,
Deuteronomy 30:15–19 uses "today" four times, insisting

that God's covenant with the Israelites will bring life if they keep it, death if they don't. This choice is faced *today*,—*today* for those Moses is addressing and *today* for later Israelites and their spiritual descendants, including ourselves, who read the account many generations later.

We "remember today" when we read Scripture attentively, alone or with others in the liturgy. Many find great help in the memories recalled in praying the rosary, which allows them to participate personally, today, in fifteen great Gospel events. The much-loved Pope John XXIII, affectionately called *il Nono Buono* (the Good Grandfather) by the Italians, used to fit into his very busy daily schedule all fifteen decades of the rosary. He writes about it in his famous *Journal*. One of his remarks is apposite here: "Someone without a knowledge of history is like a person without a memory—a very incomplete person." People of faith reciting Psalm 95, or the mysteries of the rosary, take their personal problems of today back into the perspective of history as they remember the events of the Bible. They discover that what God did then, in the Sinai desert or in Bethlehem or on Calvary, God wants to do with me and my difficulties now. Tournay says the Jews kept reciting the psalms in the desperate days of the Babylonian captivity because the psalms "worked." They were beams of light from God illuminating their seemingly hopeless prison. People who have recited the psalms with faith over the succeeding two-and-a-half millennia have made the same discovery.

13 A Tear, a Death, and a Statue

Psalm 34:6

IF SOMEONE ASKED YOU TO GIVE THE ESSENTIAL MESSAGE OF the 150 psalms in one sentence you could do a lot worse than quote Psalm 34:6: "This poor man cried and YHWH heard him." The poor one is *ani*, which as we saw before, is someone who is in distress and very conscious of possessing almost nothing except great trust in YHWH. So the person turns to YHWH in this new and almost hopeless situation—and YHWH does come once more to the rescue. Time and again in the psalms, YHWH comes to "redeem" the faithful Israelite. The Hebrew word is *go'el*, often used in the Old Testament and always referring to a blood-bond. Psalm 74:2 is an example. Psalm 19:14 calls YHWH *go'ali*, "My Redeemer." Isaiah chapters 40–55 will fully develop this concept of God our Redeemer who has "blood ties" with us.

In Psalm 34:8 the psalmist seems to sum up a lifetime of trusting in the Lord and cries out: "How good is YHWH— only taste and see!" Tasting the Lord, notes Stuhlmueller, refers to knowing by experience rather than by a merely theoretical and rational process. It's the knowledge of "connaturality" that a child has of its mother's love. The gift of knowledge is one of St Thomas Aquinas' seven gifts of the Holy Spirit, giving the recipient intuitive insights into the God who reveals himself in the Scriptures. It is the fulfillment of what the Fathers, those great saints and teachers of the first centuries of Christianity, and St Thomas Aquinas said was the central prophesy of the Old Testament. This "central Prophesy" is Jeremiah 31:31–34: "I will make a new covenant . . . deep within their hearts I will plant my law . . . no longer will they need [teachers] . . . to know YHWH. No, all, from greatest to humblest, will know me. It is YHWH who speaks." Stuhlmueller insists that we will only understand this and the inner treasures of the psalms through prayer—in prayer the Holy Spirit tells us what he means in the psalms he inspired. Jesus told Peter, in Matthew 16:17, that a disciple needs "the revelation of the Father," and not mere human reasoning, to be able to recognize the mystery of God's Kingdom at work among us. Prayer is a time when we seek the help of the Holy Spirit to understand and experience YHWH "who is making us." YHWH's revelations in the Scriptures, in the "signs of the times" happening around us and in us, in his Church and in history, are the strong colors of the spectrum of reality. They become the light by which we see clearly when they pass through the prism of authentic prayer.

Back in the fifties we used an expression that has mostly disappeared from our Catholic vocabulary. The expression has disappeared but not the reality. We used to say that certain priests preached with "unction." Unction, of course, means anointing (by the Holy Spirit). Hearers sensed that such a priest, or brother or nun, was deeply in touch with the Holy Spirit who gave him the ability to convince people about the reality and beauty of the things of God. Such a teacher has received "the gift of understanding" from the Holy Spirit, to use an expression dear to St Thomas Aquinas. Such people teach from an inner experience coming from the Holy Spirit. A parent with this gift convinces the children that God and prayer are very important. The Spirit's gift of understanding, as with all his seven gifts, is meant for every Christian. As the gift deepens, the recipient begins to understand: "How good is YHWH—only taste and see!" It is then that the psalms come alive. Your face might even begin to glow like Fr Stuhlmueller's when you talk to your children or students about the psalms and the Scriptures!

Several weeks ago in a parish church I met a couple in their late thirties who believe they experienced Psalm 34:6 quite dramatically. She has always been a true believer, takes great pride in her seven children, and wild horses would not keep her from Sunday Mass. He never had the slightest interest in her faith but loved her very much and so went to Sunday Mass to help her with the children. One Sunday, he told me, bored and wishing the priest would hurry up, he gazed absent-mindedly over the altar at the face of the Crucified. He started! A large tear welled up in Christ's eye and rolled slowly down his cheek. After Mass the husband went up and studied the ceiling. But no, there was no evidence of a leak. Maybe a swallow? No, that would have left a telltale white streak.

The next Sunday he was utterly dumbfounded when the same thing happened. Again he waited till everyone had left and tried to find a natural cause. He could not, search as he might, and he felt overwhelmed: Christ was real, just as his wife had been trying to tell him, yet for so long he had been totally disinterested in Christ's love and cruci-fixion. He enrolled in the RCIA (catechumenate) course of instructions and began attending both the Vigil Mass alone and the 10 am Mass with his family.

His wife told me she had prayed so long, and apparently so ineffectively, that he would receive the gift of faith. She had been nearing frustration at his total disinterest when the incident involving the crucifix occurred. The husband made his first move to find Christ because of the unusual occurrences but now was enjoying an experience similar to that of C. S. Lewis, who also had sought the Lord reluctantly at first. But then something wonderful and new had entered his life, as real as the experience of falling in love.

Even if someone were to discover a natural cause of the tears from the crucifix, it would not affect the husband's new faith. He now experienced the reality of Christ and longed to receive the Eucharist at Easter time when his instructions finished.

Carroll Stuhlmueller told us of a somewhat similar experience a relative of his had had going on pilgrimage to Sainte Anne de Beaupre in Quebec.

A poll taken among Australian Catholics about homilies revealed, among other things, that people like a priest becoming personal, bringing his own experiences, surprises, and failures into his homily. I have on the desk before me a kind of Psalm 34:6-letter I wrote in November, 1962, when I was "this poor man who cried to the Lord." I had been made parish priest of Takada, Nara Prefecture, Japan, with approximately 150,000 people in my parish. Seventeen people, mostly of the poorer class, came to the rickety store that was the church to greet me the Sunday I took over. Over the next few years we made little progress, numbers-wise. Bishop Furuya had instructed me, as I left for Australia on leave in 1961, to raise money and build a ferro-concrete kindergarten, "so as to make contacts with normal dwellers in the city." The cost would be £20,000 ($40,000). Friends organized slide nights, some pastors allowed me to speak in their churches, one being St Patrick's, Church Hill, Sydney.

Mrs Beatrice Baldock, of the Sydney suburb of Mosman, was in the congregation. I received an envelope from this complete stranger with a £1 ($2.00) note inside and her address on the back. In November 1962, now back in Takada, I sent a Thank You/Report to all our donors, Beatrice included. We had £14,000 ($28,000) in hand, which was wonderful, but I (man of little faith) added: "We are £6,000 ($12,000) short. Please pray for us . . . We will offer our Masses, prayers, and work on the nine days before Christmas for you, in gratitude for your generosity."

I have Beatrice's reply to me, written on December 23, 1962 saying that my letter had prompted her to buy a lottery ticket, which she called "Takada and I," promising herself to give half of any prize to the Takada kindergarten fund. "It was drawn last Friday, December 21, in the middle of the nine days of Masses and prayer, and lo and behold, the ticket won first prize, £12,000 ($24,000) . . . How do I get your £6,000 to you?" We in Takada decided God really wanted that Christian kindergarten in our city.

I have a photo on my desk of five-year-old Kimiko Hatta and her mother. They were two of a group of "poor ones who cried to the Lord," and YHWH heard in the strangest, even most terrible of ways. Early in 1968 our church council at Takada decided to borrow money, using the decrepit store-church as surety, and build the city's first Catholic church in a location that had been settled when Taima Temple was built nearby in 684 AD. The church council said to me and the assistant priest, Joe Rooney: "Let's not have a cheap plaster statue of Mary as a westerner with blue eyes and fair hair, but one harmonizing with Japanese artistic traditions." Joe and I agreed: "As a Semite she probably looked more like a Japanese than a northern European!"

We asked a young sculptor named Kosaka to give us a sketch of and a quote for a small *Nihon-teki* (Japanese-style) statue. The sketch was magnificent but the price beyond us—100,000 yen, about $3,000. We didn't answer the sculptor and he wrote again. "If I am to finish the statue for the church opening in May, I must begin soon. Making a bronze statue takes all that time. Do you want it?" I put the letter on my desk, promising myself to answer with a refusal by Sunday night, "If Our Lady doesn't come to our rescue."

Catholic Church,
Isono Higashi,
Yamato Takada City,
Nara-Ken, Japan.

November 1962.

Dear Friends of Takada,

Thanks to your gifts, this Xmas will be a happy one in Takada, Japan. As in other years, the midnight light of our "churchette" will be but a tiny candleglow in the "'encircling gloom". Our hundred voices will sing to a Christ Child who can find no room in the thirty thousand homes around us. But this Xmas we have the joy of offering the Christ Child an architect's plan — a plan of a kindergarten. and Christian Centre. This is thanks to you, "wise men from the West".

Pius XII said: 'Rise up, mobilize. To action — with courage and boldness, with an energy that will sweep along the tired, the weak, and those who no longer believe in the nobility of the Cause that they must defend.' To mobilize, will cost us £20,000 in buildings. You have given £14,000 already. Many of you promised to keep giving. So we took a bold decision, and laid a plan before this City's Administration. To gain permission, we promised to have our buildings up by Xmas 1963.

You have given Takada's little band of Christians new spirit, hope, fight. Since returning, my every sermon has been about you. Now when I speak of our world-encircling brotherhood in the Faith, it has a vivid meaning to these Japanese. They are moved when they hear the personal stories of generosity behind the £14,000. As a sign of gratitude, they asked me to send each of you a Xmas Card. They will pay the expenses, and know it is an honour. We will offer all our Masses, prayers and work on the 9 days before Xmas for you. Already, we are doing this every First Saturday.

The very first radio programme I heard on returning to Japan was from Radio Moscow — a brilliant and bitter attack on the West. The Reds won in China. They are battling to win Japan right now. We promise you to fight hard with those spiritual weapons you sent. We need your further help to get those buildings up.

Let us pray together for loyalty to Christ, for loyalty in His Brotherhood.

Paul Glynn, S. M., and Takada Christians.

FORWARDING ADDRESSES FOR GIFTS

"Harvest," 3 Mary St.
Hunter's Hill,
NS.W. AUST.
or
Box 2049, Welligton,
NEW ZEALAND

FRIDAY, 21.12.62

34

OUR
MASSES = 9 DAYS BEFORE
XMAS

M Osman
23ʳᵈ Dec SUNDAY

Dear Father,

As your Christmas
Card was the first one we
recieved. I decided to buy a
lottery ticket in aid of your
Kindergarten sharing the
prize with you. I called the
ticket "Takada & I" it was
drawn last Friday and low
and behold it won first
prize of £12.000 yours prayers
must have been very strong
What I want to know
is how to get your £6.000
to you. Will I send it
direct or perhaps you

can let me know what to
do with it
This is the cutting out
of the paper..

God's Blessing on all
your works

Sincerely
(Mrs) Beatrice Baddock

SPECIAL

The eight major prizes in Special Lottery No. 949 drawn today went to:

First: **Takada and I** synd., Mrs B. Baldock, G.P.O., Sydney.

Second: **Papa** synd., Mrs M. P. Bibb, Ocean Street, Narrabeen.

Third: **P.M.L.** synd., Miss L. Morgan, Bond Street, Mosman.

Fourth: **Xmas Greeting** synd., Mrs R. Sneezby, Alice Street, Auburn.

Fifth: **Tom and I** synd., G. D. McCutcheon, Moore Street, Drummoyne.

Sixth: **6285** synd., B.F., G.P.O., Adelaide, S.A.

Seventh: **Joint A/C** synd., A. R. Parker, Queen's Road, Hurstville.

Eighth: **10-of-us** synd., I. Brackenreg, Marion Street, Bankstown.

Major prizes were drawn by Mr A. F. Kilimoff, a visitor from New Guinea.

Prizes will be payable on and after Thursday, December 27.

I was teaching catechism that Sunday morning when Sister interrupted me. "There is a man you should see at the front door." As he introduced himself I saw that his eyes were red from crying. His daughter Kimiko, was one of the 230 children who had enrolled in our kindergarten the previous year. He said she loved the prayers Sister taught them. Each night she solemnly knelt and prayed in front of a Madonna-and-Child card before bed. "My wife said Kimiko looked so beautiful that she wanted to become a Christian and be able to pray like that. But," he continued, "I said: 'No, we are Buddhists even if we don't practice.' Some months later my job changed and we all moved to Osaka. We found a new kindergarten there for Kimiko, but after the very first day, she pouted and said it was no good—no one said any prayers there! We explained that the Takada Catholic kindergarten was special, and that most Japanese kindergarten do not say prayers.

"Last Friday Kimiko came home from her new kindergarten and stopped by workmen repairing a fault in an elevator of the 13-storey apartment building where we live. A gas cylinder they were using for acetylene welding exploded at that moment, hurling Kimiko into the far wall. They picked her up with her clothes and most of her skin off, burnt black. They telephoned me at work and I raced to the hospital and was utterly devastated when I was led to her bed. The pain killer injections weren't taking—her veins were in such a state. To stop her struggling and scratching her itching body, they had her arms and legs tied down with bandages. She looked as if she was crucified. She was whimpering for water, but the doctor said it would only make her retch. I just stood there thunderstruck behind my wife, watching Kimiko writhing in pain.

"Suddenly my wife remembered how Kimiko loved the prayers at your kindergarten. She bent down to Kimiko's ear and said 'Don't cry. Sister and the children at the Takada kindergarten are praying for you.' The effect was extraordinary. The memory of those prayers with Sister and her little classmates must have been so beautiful that it took her mind off the pain. She became quite peaceful. My wife continued speaking softly about the prayers and Kimiko remained tranquil. That's how she died. I, who stopped my wife studying your faith, have come to thank you. Because of your Christian faith our little girl died consoled and at peace!"

He took an envelope from the pocket and handed it to me. "I want you to build swings or something in her memory." Japanese write on the outside of the envelope the sum of the donation they are giving. 100,000 yen was written! I told him of the statue of Mary and that the decision had to be made that day. Could we use the donation for that instead of swings? He agreed immediately.

Kimiko's mother was present as we unveiled the statue when the new church was blessed by Bishop Furuya on May 26, 1968. On the back of the bronze statue of a poorly-clad, somewhat emaciated and travel-worn Mary leading the Christ Child back from Egypt across the Gaza desert, is the inscription: In memory of Kimiko Hatta, taken to heaven, aged six years. At the opening ceremony we gave Kimiko's mother a large photo of the statue. Some weeks later she wrote: "The holy picture of Mary and the Christ Child which Sister gave Kimiko when she first went to your kindergarten is pretty, with lovely colors. But I like the photo you gave me of the new bronze statue much better. Mary is crossing a desert and she and her child look worn-out. That is like me just now. I look at this statue and am strengthened. My husband and I were all the more devastated by Kimiko's death because she was our only child. Now the doctor has just confirmed I am going to have another child!"

On the Friday the accident occurred, our kindergarten teachers were having a cup of green tea after the children had gone home, and one of them switched on the television for the late-afternoon news flash. They were startled to learn of Kimiko's accident and had gone straight to the chapel to pray for her. One of the senior teachers, Kyoko Kubo, said at our next weekly meeting: "Sometimes I have been sad that we work so hard and yet so few parents are interested in baptism. Kimiko's terrible but beautiful death tells me that God is at work in our lives in a way far beyond our tiny understanding."

14 Like a Swallow's Homing Instinct

The Zion Psalms

A GOOD TWENTY-FIVE YEARS AGO U.S. PRIEST AND SOCIOLOGIST Thomas Newbold came to Japan and gave missionaries a memorable summer school. He warned us that we would be hard put to last as missionaries if we were perfectionists who demanded as a right a tidy parish, diocese, etc. He told us a riddle that, he said, "comes from the Middle Ages and is good theology." It goes: Why is the Church like Noah's Ark? Answer: If it wasn't for the storm outside none of us would put up with all the stinks inside!

The previous chapter was about the very personal dimension in many psalms: "This poor man cried out and the Lord heard him." It seems the original basis of many psalms was a written prayer of gratitude, for instance for personal deliverance from unjust enemies, left behind by some worshipper as a kind of offering of thanks at the temple. Priests or levites saw it, kept it, later modified it, and, lo! eventually it became one of the 150 Psalms. Many psalms are very personal and subjective and they became official psalms only when taken up by the temple community. The Psalm scholars tell us that most psalms found final form when modified to become part of the chanted (and often acted) temple liturgies. Judaism was not a God-and-me spirituality that bred spiritual Lone Rangers. The center of gravity was the covenant, which was made between YHWH and the Jewish community, the People of

God. There is no doubt that a dogma-less, a church-less religion, has a strong appeal, above all in our age where self-fulfillment is all the go. Dorothy Sayers once said: "Any stigma is good enough to beat a dogma with!" Towards the end of the last century, famous Japanese convert Kanzo Uchimura, after going to the United States in the first flush and simplicity of his new Christian faith, was so confused and demoralized by the many competing forms of American Christianity that he returned to Japan and formed Mukyokai (No-Church) Christianity. The odors of Noah's Ark have caused many like him to say: I love Christ but hate the denominations! Many Japanese intellectuals joined Mukyokai only to later leave it. Something biblical and human was missing.

The psalms belong unequivocally to "denominational" Judaism. They center on the temple and liturgical worship. Five psalms, for instance, include the words "under the shadow of his wings"—a term meaning the temple, because of the two cherubim whose wings outstretched over the Ark in the temples' Holy of Holies (Pss 17:8; 36:7; 57:1; 91:4). Psalm 61:4 has a double reference to the temple: "Let me stay in your tent forever, finding protection under the shelter of your wings." The Ark of the Covenant, God's "seat," was kept in a tent during the Exodus journey. John's Gospel, in describing the Eternal Word becoming man, resurrects Israel's primitive and beautiful memory of the temple as a travelling tent: "The Word . . . dwelt among us" is, literally translated, "He pitched his tent among us."

Nineteen psalms refer explicitly to Zion. (Sion is another form of writing Zion, the two names being interchangeable.) Zion was the rocky hill on which King David built his palace after he dislodged the Jebusites from their fortress. When David had the Ark of the Covenant brought to what had been called the City of David, it became known as "the City of God." David's son Solomon built the temple on the same rocky hill (sometimes given the grander title of mountain), and Zion came to mean the temple. Psalm 24 was chanted at the annual commemoration of Solomon enthroning the Ark in the temple on Mount Zion. YHWH "left his home in heaven" to live in the Jerusalem temple! That stupendous fact is why the temple became the center of Jewish faith and devotion. Over succeeding centuries splinter groups and schismatics broke away from the mainstream, setting up rival centers. The psalms never recognized these as anything but false pretenders. The psalms kept asserting: From Zion (the temple) flow YHWH's blessings.

Psalms 46 and 48 are Zion psalms. Psalm 46:1–3 is an affirmation of total trust in the God who has come to live in Jerusalem. Using old cosmic images of the primal creation struggle, it asserts that even though surrounding kingdoms, dynasties, and cultures tumble, Jerusalem (and so Israel) will be secure. "Mountains tumble to the bottom of the seas as the Waters [of Chaos] rage and roar." Ah yes, but "YHWH is on our side. He has made Jerusalem an impregnable citadel. His presence has tamed the Waters of Chaos and from them made a stream that refreshs the City of God." In actual fact the hard limestone base of Zion had yielded to receive the gentle flow of the waters of Shiloah that came from the spring of Gihon outside the city and were vital when Jerusalem was besieged on all sides. Isaiah 8:6 sees "the waters of Shiloah that flow in tranquility" as a lovely symbol of God's gracious presence. But when Jerusalem rejects this grace and seeks salvation in military strength, political alliances, or intrigue, there is a terrible implosion of the Waters of Chaos: ". . . the mighty and deep waters . . . will overflow . . . bursting banks . . . flowing over the whole breadth of your land, Immanuel" (Isa 8:7–8).

Psalm 46:5 continues: "God is within the city—she can never be defeated!" Neighboring kingdoms might totter and nations rage but when YHWH's voice sounds out everything fades away. ". . . He puts an end to warfare on all sides, destroying bow . . . and spear" (v. 9). There is a great message from YHWH to Jerusalem: "Be still and know that I am God" (v. 10). These are beautiful words, assuring Israelites they need not fear the powerful, militaristic nations surrounding tiny Judah. This promise and prophesy gave wonderful confidence until Jerusalem was totally destroyed by Babylon in 587 BC and Rome in AD 70! How could Jewish faith survive such a betrayal of a solemn Bible oath? A crucial question, to be taken up a little later—first let us examine some other Zion Psalms.

Psalm 48 probably originated after the Assyrian king Sennacherib's mighty army surround Jerusalem in 701 BC. Just when the city seemed like a helpless plum about to be plucked by Sennacherib, he inexplicably withdrew his army and the city was saved. This deepened Jewish convictions that the Holy City would never fall. Psalm 48 praises Jerusalem as "the city of our God YHWH, beautiful and the joy of the whole earth . . . God himself is her fortress." Zion is situated "deep in the heart of the North" (according to the pre-Israelite Ugaritic myths the chief god Baal-Hadad dwelt in the mountains of the north— once again YHWH's revelation responds to human yearnings to draw close to the Source.) Psalm 48:8 and 12 tell us: See for yourselves this city, humanly helpless before Sennacherib. Yet it stands intact. Go through its streets, count its watch towers, feel the strength of its walls. Yes, God's promises to protect his city always are as solid as the rock on which the city is built.

Psalm 50:1–2 tells us "YHWH, God of gods, summons the whole earth from east to west and speaks. From Zion, perfection of beauty, he shines forth." In verses 3–4 Zion becomes the new Sinai, the desert mountain where YHWH spoke intimately to Moses in "consuming fire and raging storm" (see Ex 19:16–19).

Psalm 65 begins: "Praise is our due to you in Zion, O

God." Verse 4 speaks of the blessedness of believers who have been invited "into your courts . . . into the temple which is your house, O God." In verse 7, YHWH calms the raging of those Waters of Chaos. To people without the vision of faith, it might seem that the powerful waters escape YHWH's hands: violent downpours tear down hill-sides and flood the land (v 10). But these storms prove to be the prelude to "singing crops of wheat." Verse 2 was right: God hears those prayers said in Zion's temple!

Psalm 68:17 is full of power: "Escorted by thousands of myriads of divine chariots"—Pharaoh's inadequate chari-ots rust at the bottom of the sea—"the Lord left Sinai for his sanctuary." Verses 24–28 give a charming vignette of the Jerusalem liturgy, cantors marching at the head of the temple procession, closely followed by musicians and maidens playing tambourines. The choir strikes up, and into view come the legendary tribes, each with a robed prince at its head. The psalm concludes with: "The God of Israel is in his sanctuary, giving power and strength to his people" (v. 35). A. A. Anderson comments that YHWH's "power to save is not simply an eschatological [end of the world] expectation but a present reality experienced through participation in the cultus [the Temple liturgy]." This is one of Stuhlmueller's key teachings; the psalms (and the liturgy) become real when you begin to experi-ence now the past salvation marvels of the YHWH you are "remembering"—when you realize that the power he has shown in the past is just as present and effective today. Believers can experience it in the temple liturgy.

Psalm 76:2 again tells us that "God has pitched his tent in Salem" (another name for Jerusalem) and "his home is in Zion." Beautiful Psalm 84 is a poem of a pilgrim on the road yearning for Jerusalem and the temple. Israel's liturgy was full of remembered journeys—Abraham's journey to unknown destinations, the desert journey from Egypt to the Promised Land under Moses, journeys of prophets like

Elijah, Jeremiah, and Jonah and the fifteen or more psalms composed for the three annual pilgrim journeys to Jerusalem. Stuhlmueller calls them "symbols of the interior journey to the depths of oneself" that every real believer must make. Palm 84, like other "Sons of Korah" Psalms, is a yearning to be back home in the temple. It "pines" for "your house, YHWH . . . your courts and altars." The swallows darting in and out of the sacred building inspire the psalmist's reverie: the swallows' God-given instincts bring them home from the long flight south in autumn, to find a safe place to nest in spring. But the gracious Lord has granted something greater to the psalmist—a house, a very home in the temple-home of YHWH! The psalmist sings this lovely song as he and thousands of other travel-weary pilgrims arrive in Jerusalem and go straight to the temple. "A single day in your courts" is worth the long, hard journey ("a thousands days"), for there we "stand on the steps of God's house" (v. 10). There were hardships and dangers aplenty on the pilgrim journey ("going through the Valley of the Weeper" in verse 6, the origin of the expression "this vale of tears" in that prayer our pioneer forebears loved, "Hail Holy Queen"). Dangers will be there on the journey back home, too, but YHWH is "a shield . . . conferring grace . . . to those who walk in sincerity of heart . . . who put their trust in you" (vv. 11–12). This is a love song for the ancient psalmist and the millions of spiritual descendants who have recited it ever since.

One male parishioner in Ars, when St John Vianney was its pastor, was sure he was on a pilgrim journey Home but maybe didn't know Psalm 84. However, the experience that gave birth to the psalm was well known to him. This nondescript old parishioner would sit for hours most days in the church where the Blessed Sacrament was present. John Vianney asked him what he did there and marveled at the husky reply: "I looks at Him and He looks at me."

I suppose there's a healthy side to the media's seeming

fury in exposing the sins of organized religion, but journalists sometimes go on, in a none-too-ingenuous way, to
suggest that all religion is pathetic, or even pathological. I
wish they would visit some parish churches for Sunday
Mass instead of just trundling out intellectual arguments
or anecdotes suggesting that no one can be certain of anything supernatural or even of God's existence, let alone
Christ's resurrection. They would meet so many there,
intellectuals and otherwise, who meet YHWH regularly
and are steadied and guided by him every week in the
community liturgy—and often during the week at daily
Mass, or just sitting there like the old peasant in Ars.

15 Zion, Mother of Many Nations, and the Pilgrim Psalms

T HERE ARE SO MANY ZION PSALMS THAT ONE CHAPTER CANNOT cover them. Many regard Psalm 87 as the most extraordinary. A great lover and student of the psalms, Fr Cyril Martindale, wrote that Psalm 87 is so "transcendent and sublime a vision and prophesy" that (uncharacteristically) he found himself "almost speechless." He went on: "It displays Jerusalem in its most universal, mystical aspect. The Holy Land becomes co-extensive with the world!"

The psalm opens: "YHWH loving his city that is built on the sacred mountain, chose Zion before all other cities in Jacob. O City of God, he makes wonderful prophecies about you! 'I will add Egypt and Babylon to those who recognize me. They will tell of Philistines, people of Tyre, and Ethiopians being born here [in Jerusalem]. Of Zion it will be said, everyone was born there.'" This is an extraordinary prophesy, all the more so given the intense nationalism of the Chosen People and their attitude to "the nations"—especially those who had harried and persecuted them. No doubt this is why Psalm 87 was a rather neglected one until it was embraced very enthusiastically by convert Gentile Christians. In the original Hebrew (kept in some modern translations) the synonym, the Jewish nickname for Egypt, is used. Rahab—originally the fearful Beast, the Leviathan, the Serpent that dwelt in the Waters of Chaos. The Holy City was chosen and protected by YHWH as the fortified citadel and rallying place for those who wish to be his allies in the fight against chaos in all its forms.

For most Israelites, the thought of rapacious Babylonians becoming children of YHWH was so unacceptable that they interpreted the psalm to mean Jews born in Babylon, that is Diaspora Jews. Early Christian converts, however, saw the psalm as a spiritual fulfillment of Ezechiel 38:12, proclaiming Jerusalem as "the navel of the earth." Psalm 87:5–7 insists: "All [believers] are born in Jerusalem!" The polyglot Christians rejoiced in this citizenship of the mystical Jerusalem, unrestricted by geography or race. The destruction of Jerusalem four decades after Christ's death did not destroy in these new converts faith in biblical guarantees that Jerusalem would never be destroyed! It was the same with scriptural promises about the Temple. Paul in 2 Corinthians 6:16, for instance, had assured them that the indwelling of the Holy Spirit made them God's living Temples! Almighty God, who had created time and space, had freed the Holy City and its temple from the limitations of place.

Fr Martindale was quoted earlier in connection with Psalm 87. A classical Englishman, he arrived to study at Harrow just after Winston Churchill left. Going onto Oxford he took first class honors in the Humanities. Turning down the chance to continue on teaching Greco-Roman classics at the university, he became a Jesuit priest. A convert to the faith himself, Martindale would lead a great number into that faith over the years, from intellectuals to working class folks. He wrote many books about faith and "the realities of the supernatural," and was in much demand as a lecturer and radio broadcaster in England and abroad. Quite deeply moved by the confusion co-existing with a yearning for reality among many students and not a few professors (C. S. Lewis for instance), Martindale did a great deal of work on the Oxford campus.

However, he also spent much time among the poor in London's East End, where he set up clubs and associations to help slum dwellers retain their human dignity.

Martindale could have led a lucrative life in Oxford's ivory towers but chose to use his brilliant, wide-ranging, and disciplined mind especially to teach common folk, ordinary, struggling citizens. He had a consuming love of France's pilgrim city, Lourdes. He saw a magnificent fulfillment of Psalm 87 in the millions who went there each year as pilgrims, speaking a hundred languages but marching together in the mighty procession and singing in one tongue the haunting chorus, "Ave, Ave, Ave Maria." He loved the great crowds, often in distinctive national dress, with thousands of nurses, doctors, and brancardiers coming each year to attend the pathetic streams of sick and dying pilgrims. He never tired of writing and speaking of the extraordinary peace of heart pervading the city. He discovered in the miracle cures cataloged by the international group of professors and doctors at the Medical Bureau both scientific proofs of the supernatural realities and the footprints of the Galilean Healer and his Mother still walking among us. Brave the sceptic who publicly ridiculed Lourdes miracles when Martindale was around! He had a great love of liturgy, both of the Old Temple in Jerusalem and of the New. His books on the Mass attest to his grasp of its theology and to the energy he gained from his daily Eucharist.

In his book, *The Sweet Singer of Israel*, you see how the psalms also energized Martindale—and how he found in his new faith (and his beloved England's old faith) the fulfillment of all the psalmists' yearning, pining, and trusting, and of their faith that the prophecies would one day come to fruition. It saddened him to think that for some priests the psalms in their daily prayer, the Divine Office (or breviary), became "burdensome or an affair of routine." He wrote *The Sweet Singer of Israel* (which was a name given to King David) to help them, and the growing number of lay people who were praying the psalms, to discover in them "the treasure buried in a field."

There is one more group of psalms that could be called Zion Psalms, though the official title given them in most Bibles is "Songs of Ascent," from the custom of pilgrims going up (ascending) to the Holy City on Mount Zion. These are the fifteen psalms from 120 to 134, which in all probability were composed to be sung on the three annual pilgrimages up to Jerusalem. Exodus 23:14–19 outlines the obligation to celebrate three annual feasts in the Holy City. First, that of Unleavened Bread (also called Passover), held at the time of the barley harvest (March/April). Jews "going up" to celebrate this feast remembered their ancestors' journey from Egypt under Moses. Secondly the Feast of Weeks (or Pentecost, meaning the fiftieth day after Passover), held at the time of the all-important wheat harvest (May/June). Thirdly, the Feast of Tabernacles or Booths, but better called Huts, held at the time of ingathering the grape and olive harvests (September/October). Leviticus 23:33–43 tells the people to live in temporary huts for the seven days of the feast, remembering the way their ancestors lived on the move when escaping from Egyptian slavery. If you have been in Jerusalem for this picturesque feast you would have seen huts erected here and there in the city, observant believers dwelling in them.

The fifteen Pilgrim Psalms, which are revealed as more and more beautiful the more you study and pray them, leave one, like Martindale, wanting to remain speechless. Two themes run through them: We are on a journey, with its hardships and dangers, but we are journeying to the sacred dwelling place of the Lord who loves us. In a way they are like classical Japanese haiku poems. The greatest haiku evocatively counterpoise Buddhism's two great themes, the transience of everything created and the permanence of Absolute Mercy. There are moving examples among haiku by Kobayashi Issa and Matsuo Basho.

This book is meant to be an appetizer, a stimulant to lead you to a thorough and, if possible, ongoing study of the psalms through the eyes of great commentators like Stuhlmueller. So without attempting the impossible task of summarizing the fifteen Pilgrim Psalms, I'll attempt a few salient points. First, they are simple gems like Beethoven's Pastoral Symphony. Psalm 121: "I lift my eyes to the mountains [the Jerusalem mountains coming into sight after the long journey on foot]. Where do I find help? Ah, my help comes from YHWH, who made heaven and earth . . . This guardian of yours does not fall asleep, and will not let your feet slip . . ." Psalm 122: "How I was filled with joy when the word went about, 'we are going (on pilgrimage) to the house of the Lord.'" Then, after reaching Jerusalem:

> And now our feet rest in your gateways, Jerusalem, city restored [after the Babylonian destruction]. Rebuilt, and united again! The tribes of YHWH have come up to praise him as he instructed Israel . . . Pray for peace, peace in Jerusalem and prosperity in your homes. Pray for peace within the city walls, prosperity within your homes and palaces. All here are my brethren, my friends, and so I say: "Peace be with you." YHWH our God lives here and so I pray for his gifts for all of you.

Psalm 123 was probably written when the Israelites were either under total foreign domination or at least were vassals to some oppressive overlord. They were humiliated but the psalm tells them to lift up their hearts:

> Slaves must watch the hands of their masters and mistresses, ready to move at the slightest command or receive a blow. Yes, we live in this despicable condition but if we

lift our eyes beyond our masters to the Lord we recover our dignity and courage. He, unlike a slavemaster, is gracious and will always help us when we turn to him.

So often in their long and heroic history Jews living in Jerusalem, Judea, or in the Diaspora suffered under harsh masters. But the Jews who clung to their belief in YHWH retained their pride and sense of worth because they kept remembering that YHWH was their loving Father. The Africans who were brought as slaves to the United States picked up this message from the psalms. The songs they created known as "spirituals," are beautiful testimony to that.

Psalm 124 begins: "If YHWH had not been on our side." These words are pure gold when you understand they are from Genesis 31:42. This is what Jacob, when in exile, said to his taskmaster Laban, who had prevented his return to the Promised Land for fourteen years.

Jacob is a key figure in the Old Testament. His momentous life took up fourteen pages of Genesis beginning at chapter 25, a life crisscrossed with long and arduous journeys. He is a man ever in conflict. His bitter opposers include his father Isaac, his murderous twin Esau, and his father-in-law Laban. His son Ruben commits incest with his stepmother, his daughter Dinah is abducted by Shechem and raped. Jacob's sons wreak a terrible vengeance for that, deceiving all the men in that town and slaughtering them. Jacob had to flee for his life. And we think we have troubles!

In one of the Old Testament's most bizarre passages Jacob is attacked by an unknown assailant in the depths of the night. Jacob struggles desperately until daybreak when he receives a heavy blow in the thigh. In an extraordinary climax to the story we learn that the attacker is YHWH who rewards Jacob with a special blessing and a new name, Israel.

A Jew reading Jacob's famous words in the first verse of Psalm 124 understood the implications of this Pilgrim Psalm. It will enrich our reciting of the psalms if we get in touch with them too. Faithful Jews chanting it on the long and often dangerous pilgrimage to Jerusalem knew they were on the same journey of faith as Jacob, and as Abraham, Moses, Elijah, and all their great ancestors. The journey is a tough one. The psalm speaks of its dangers— being burnt alive, being swallowed up by the terrible waters, being caught in the net (of the trapper). It is the same for us. The risks are great but to refuse them and the journey is to refuse to become what God meant us to be. It is to opt for the safety of chicken wire and a muddy yard rather than rise up to the buffeting winds of the mountains and the overall vision they give. A hen or an eagle, that's the choice we each must make. Pilgrim travellers or sedentary couch potatoes!

Psalm 128 says "we will be happy if we walk in his ways." Ways, roads, and journeys crisscross the Bible, and not only the Bible. The name of one of ancient China's great philosophical religions, Tao, means the Way, the Path. This is *Do* (or *To*) in Japanese, found, for instance, in Shinto (the way of kami), Chado (the way of tea), Kendo (the way of fencing), and Judo (the way of self-defence). Japanese gardens usually have stepping stones placed irregularly, forcing you to take deliberate steps. This is to make you consciously choose the path, the way. No matter how difficult, a journey is bearable, even joyful if it has a worthwhile destination. Viktor Frankl, the Viennese depth analyst, made a great discovery when he was sent to Auschwitz: people's powers of resistance are greatly increased if they have something precious to live for. He survived the horrors of the camp and gave Logotherapy to psychiatry, Logo(s) meaning spiritual meaning. Life's journey, however painful, acquires meaning if there is a worthwhile destination. In the second century BC, when belief in an afterlife and heaven for the just came into Jewish belief, the pilgrim journeys to Jerusalem became both a part of and symbolic of the believers' journey Home, to the New Jerusalem and life with God forever.

Among Vatican II's keynote expressions are "the pilgrim People of God . . . the pilgrim Church." Like the Jews under Moses, we have to cross deserts to gain our final freedom. We become footsore and travel-grimy. At moments of weariness we stumble and sometimes fall. But it is all very worthwhile because beyond the last stony desert and rugged mountain is the Beatific Vision, the participation in God's happiness. The title of the final section of Vatican II's Constitution on the Church is: "Mary, a Sign of Sure Hope and of Solace for God's People in Pilgrimage."

The Mary of the Gospels is a woman of journeys—to Bethlehem, to Jerusalem, to Ain Karim visiting Elizabeth, to dark Calvary, to the Upper room at Pentecost. Fittingly the Pilgrim Psalms are used in the Divine Office for her feasts. Catholic (and Orthodox) history, past and present, is rich in instances of Mary coming to aid people who sought her help. Cathedral shrines like Notre Dame in Paris, wayside statuettes in Southern Germany, her images in Australian kitchens, rosaries in coalminer's pockets . . . all give testimony to this.

Five million visit her shrine at Lourdes each year because they experience a heavenly peace there. Mary appeared to the first pilgrim, young Bernadette Soubirous, on February 11, 1858, and over subsequent weeks spoke of the happiness of heaven—Bernadette said that the great beauty and radiance of "the Lady" convinced her beyond any need of words. You can see in the famous Medical Bureau at Lourdes fully documented accounts of miraculous healings, signed by batteries of famous medical professors and specialists.

Those accounts draw some searching agnostics to

Lourdes but the majority of pilgrims are ordinary people who have sought God and his will for most of their lives. They come in response to Mary's call for pilgrimages of prayer and penance. Some of the latter-day gnostics scoff at "the ignorant plebs" and the cheap Lourdes souvenirs they carry home—often cheap because it took the rest of their money to get there! But what's the use of having an expensive collection of memorabilia if you don't know the peace of kneeling in prayer before an image of Mary. Josh Billings said: "It ain't the folks that don't know what worries me. It's the folks that don't know they don't know."

I've heard sophisticated moderns attack Lourdes, Fatima, and more recently, Medugorje, because the apparitions always happen to children, and poorly educated children at that! Maybe this is part of Mary's message. Her son had a lot to say about becoming like a child. Pilgrim Psalm 131 is about a wise adult who has achieved real peace in the discovery of what Paul Ricoeur beautifully calls the "second childhood of the spirit." The psalm begins with a series of negatives: "Lord, my heart is not proud, nor my eyes haughty, I busy not myself with grand affairs nor marvelous things beyond my ability." Stuhlmueller comments: "These negatives indicate an adult who has reached quiet confidence after a long struggle . . . He now rejects his earlier propensity to venture into the mysterious ways of God as though to understand and control them." Verse 2 reads: "But I have calmed and quieted my soul, like a child quieted at its mother's breast, like a child that is quieted is my soul." Then the conclusion: "Israel, trust in YHWH, now and for always." Biblical second childhood, comments Stuhlmueller, "is not debasing. Rather it manifests the patient, strong, appreciative, and listening stance of an adult who has learned much over the years . . ." You only achieve that tranquility of heart, he concludes, if you have learned the discipline of seeking and waiting for the Lord, praying and rejoicing to discover the goodness of other people around you.

Karl Rahner, who died in 1984, was one of the great minds of this century. His monumental theological writings will surely be quoted for many generations to come. He did not just study theology, he prayed much. If you read what he wrote about prayer you soon sense that this man loved and practiced what he was writing about. Several years before he died, "the old master" wrote a touching article on the love of Jesus. Like the man who composed Psalm 131, the elderly Rahner could, without any embarrassment, look back on a life of acclaimed scholarship and find his greatest satisfaction in praying "like a child quieted at its mother's breast."

Here Rahner seems so different from Hans Küng. The latter is certainly a theological and scriptural popularizer, but that can be a dangerous profession if the popularizer is not a pray-er. Küng's writings don't seem to give his readers the sense that here is a man who prays humbly before he writes volubly! Cardinal Suenens, one of the main driving forces at Vatican II once expressed to Rahner concern about the fall-off in devotion to Mary among modern Catholics. Rahner replied: "So many Christians today have made Christ into an ideology, a *Weltanschauug*, a vision of the mind, an abstraction. Abstractions don't need a mother!" Rahner said what Stuhlmueller kept insisting on. You will only experience the spiritual energy of the psalms if you pray, if you "seek his face," if you look into YHWH's eyes and humbly ask him for the experience of Matthew 11:25: Christ blesses the Father for hiding the mysteries of the Kingdom from those handicapped by total satisfaction in their own cleverness and for *revealing* them to mere children. God is a "powerful, irreducible mystery" and we need his revelation to understand both him and his revelations in Scripture. Psalm 36:10 puts it: "In your light we see light."

Martindale saw a fulfillment of the great prophecy in Zion Psalm 87 in the liturgies of tens of thousands at

Lourdes. A Protestant has written a best-seller on Lourdes and sees the shrine as both a continuation and a fulfillment of the Pilgrim Psalms. Ruth Cranston had a longtime fascination with the modern question: Do the miraculous healings we read of in the Scripture happen today? For many people, she knew, that can be rephrased: Did miraculous healings ever happen? She traveled much in America and other countries researching this. Then she heard of Lourdes, borrowed books about it and set out herself in 1953. As she spoke fluent French she studied "miraculous cures" accepted by the famous Medical Bureau there. She then went off to interview in person those claimed to be cured and to check their stories with their doctors and the various hospitals that had issued the X-rays, temperature charts, testimonies, etc., that she had studied at the Lourdes Medical Bureau. She returned time and again to Lourdes, interviewed many of those cured who return each year to attend to sick pilgrims. She also prayed much. In the final chapter of her extensive book *The Mystery of Lourdes* (1956), Cranston quotes an American radio poll that asked: What is the major modern anxiety? More than 20,000 answered: A solid spiritual and moral basis, something I can really be sure of, or words to that effect. Cranston says Lourdes' importance lies here: miracles at Lourdes prove that God exists.

A woman who has read Christian literature very widely, Cranston complains that many "higher" biblical critics have very effectively encouraged doubt about essential teachings of the bible. Biblical miracles become mere allegories, God and the risen Jesus fall and disappear by their gnostic wayside. With this increasing cynicism about the Scriptures, moderns increasingly dismiss absolute values and moral principles, she laments. But every year millions of "the people" vote with their feet, pilgrim feet, and go to Lourdes to pray and to penance as the Gospels tell us. Thee humble pilgrims include illustrious university professors who serve voluntarily at the Medical Bureau, and other famous people who rejoice in being simple believers. Like the peasants, miners, nurses, truck drivers, and office workers they join the 150,000-strong evening processions of many tongues, and sing the joyful yet pleading Lourdes hymn to the Virgin Mother. They have arrived home, writes Cranston, in Zion:

> They looked for a city . . . a city which has foundations—foundations of love and devotion and unselfishness, genuine friendship, caring for people—whose builder and maker is God.

16 The Priest-King Messiah

THE PROTESTANT THEOLOGIAN JÜRGEN MOLTMANN, WHEN guest speaker at the 1972 International Eucharistic Congress held in Melbourne, made one point with especial emphasis: God's promises in the Bible always mean more than meets the eye. For instance the wandering Israelites were promised a land "flowing with milk and honey." If you've been to Israel, he commented, you will know it's mostly a land of stones and sand. However, the promise is magnificently true *spiritually*. The tiny land has produced bumper crops of prophets, mystics, saints, and the profound people who wrote the Bible. If you interpret everything in the Bible literally (another word could be materialistically), you get yourself into all kinds of strife and contradictions.

In the Zion Psalms YHWH promised that Jerusalem and the temple would be his home forever. Not unreasonably, the Jews interpreted this to mean that the city and temple would never be destroyed. Psalm 125 states this plainly: Zion is "unshakeable, standing forever." The cyclone from Babylon leveled both the city and the temple and faithful Jews were stunned. *En masse* they were force marched off across the Syrian desert to become captives of the Mesopotamians. The priest Ezechiel, who had warned the people before Jerusalem fell, rallied their spirits in Babylon with his mighty vision: he saw YHWH traveling to be with his captive people in Babylon. In a subsequent vision he was transported in spirit to Israel and saw the future temple as the source of spring waters that would make Israel fertile again and of fruit trees bearing monthly with leaves that were medicinal. Those miraculous waters would make the Dead Sea wholesome again, filled with fish like the Great Sea (the Mediterranean). Ezechiel's prophecy is about the Messianic era to come.

Nathan in 2 Samuel 7:10–16 pronounces the first "Royal Messianic" prophecy. The Israelites will "dwell undisturbed and forever" in the Holy Land. The royal Davidic line will never die out, "always secure before me [the Lord], your throne established for all time." These divine promises became part of Israel's faith, accepted by believing Jews as absolutely certain. Psalm after psalm hallows the prophecies, reiterates them, expands them.

The first Royal Messianic psalm, accepted wholeheartedly as such and of vital import in late Old Testament Judaism, is Psalm 2. It begins with "the nations" plotting a revolt "against YHWH and his Anointed One [i.e. Messiah]." But YHWH laughs at this human fatuity and futility, "strikes them with panic," and proclaims: "This is my king, installed by me on Zion, my holy mountain." YHWH declares this anointed king "is my Son . . . I, his father." YHWH promises him the nations, to the very ends of the earth, as his heritage. The Messiah-King will shatter rivals as naturally as a potter smashes those vessels that turn out defective.

Stuhlmueller points out how significant it is that the first two psalms in the psalter state plainly and boldly the two cardinal beliefs of the Jews at the time the psalter was given its final form after the return from Babylon. Psalm 1 is all about the Law, the "Torah." In Hebrew Torah means "instruction" rather than "legislation"—it is a much broader, richer, and encouraging concept than the legalistic-sounding term "Law." Psalm 2 is all about the

Messianic King to come. Torah and Messiah became the head and the heart of Jewish faith and hope.

Psalm 45 says extraordinary things about the Davidic Messiah-King: "of all men most handsome . . . inconquerable warrior . . . your throne lasting forever . . . anointed by God above all rivals . . . his sons will be lords of the whole world . . . nations praising his immortalized name for ever and ever."

Psalm 72 describes the Davidic king so exuberantly as "to break the bonds of all human hopes" (Stuhlmueller). The king of Jerusalem will

> defend the poorest, save the needy . . . be as welcome as rain on dry soil, and endure like the sun and the moon, age after age . . . In his reign justice and universal peace will flourish until the moon shines no more . . . The beast [Leviathan] will cower before him . . . He will feed the poor . . . for whom grain will flourish as far up as the mountaintops . . . and as abundant as grass.

The psalm concludes the hope that "every race in the world be blessed in him," and it praises YHWH who "alone performs such marvels."

Psalm 89, a truly mighty psalm celebrated in a well-known modern Christian hymn, reiterates YHWH's immutable choice of David as his "hero" (v. 19). David's dynasty, set up by the Lord as an essential part of his covenant with Israel (v. 3) will "last forever, outlasting time." The psalm surges on, a kind of Beethoven's Ninth Symphony of the Royal Messianic Psalms. The claims for David's line are so fantastic that the psalm is either the composition of an unbalanced fanatic or so glorious a prophecy as to render the believer almost speechless with awe and gratitude. Yet, from verse 38 on the great symphony becomes discordant and changes to a dirge. The reality of the Davidic line is as inglorious as the previous promises were glorious! The House of Windsor's recent *annus horribilis* is a mere summer sneeze compared to the Davidic degradation, or rather, complete dissolution. The psalm was given its final form after Babylon had wiped out the Davidic line. It is good to recite it as one of those faithful Jews living two millennia ago, feeling the near-unbearable tension they experienced as they recited prophecies that were mocked by realities. Nine times the psalm assures them of YHWH's utter fidelity to his promises, using those covenant words *hesed we'emet*, his love and fidelity. And yet the reality before their eyes! That tension between belief and appearance must have also been very difficult for people like Zachary, Elizabeth, Anna, Simeon, Simon who would one day become Peter, and yes, Mary of Nazareth, when the evil, alien Herod sat on Israel's throne aping God's anointed king.

The fierce insistence in the psalms that David's line will last forever has an equally strong response in the prophets—Amos 3:5; 9:11; Jeremiah 30:8–9, Ezechiel 30:12, etc. These forceful, absolute promises were the watershed of the two cardinal beliefs of faithful Jews just before the birth of Christ: The Torah (Psalm 1) and the Davidic Messiah-King of Zion (Psalm 2).

Psalm 132 was originally pre-Babylon, written for the exuberant liturgy commemorating how King David and all the people brought up the sacred Ark of the Covenant from Kiriath-jearim, about 10 kilometers due east. They joyfully installed it in what was now the Holy City. When Solomon built the grand and beautiful temple the liturgical procession commemorating the latter would have been magnificent, filling every Jew with honest nationalistic pride. The psalm assures them their city and land are invincible. "For YHWH has chosen Zion, desiring this to be his home . . . Here I will stay forever . . . Here I will make a horn sprout for David and trim a lamp for my anointed . . . His enemies I will cover with shame but his royal crown will flower" (v. 13,14,17). After Babylon this psalm became one of the Pilgrim Psalms. Imagine Jews coming on pilgrimage from Babylon, Greece, Carthage, and Rome when these nations were at the height of their power. What a contrast between political realities and the psalms' assurances! Yet the Jews, despoiled of power and even of their own Holy Land kept reciting Psalm 132 and coming on pilgrimage to the defaced, enfeebled Holy City, believing beyond appearances. These *anawim*, poor but with total trust in YHWH, were being prepared to accept an even greater contradiction: that God would become a man and that the great essential of their faith—that YHWH is one—would be transformed. YHWH would be revealed to be three!

I would like now to look in some detail, at the risk of being overly long-winded, at Royal Messianic Psalm 110. This psalm is especially important for Christians because it is quoted more than any other psalm in the New Testament, over thirty times. One of these cases is when Jesus tells his listeners "with ears to hear" that he himself is the psalm's fulfillment.

Psalm 110 was originally written for the coronation of a Davidic king. Stuhlmueller and A. A. Anderson regard this psalm as one of the oldest in the psalter, maybe close to the time of King David himself. Over the following five centuries it underwent editing; phrases were left out and others added. Alexander the Great set out to unite Greek and Eastern culture. He was only thirty-three years old when he died in 323 BC, the front of his body covered with scars, for he refused to lead his troops from the rear. However he had partially fulfilled his dream to unite the world via the Greek language and culture. Jews of the Diaspora began to use Greek enthusiastically and by 250 BC those living in Alexandria had completed the Greek translation of the Old Testament known as the Septuagint. There are differences between the Hebrew text used by Jews at the time of Christ and the Greek text of the Septuagint. Scholars are not certain which is more faithful to the original. This confusion, and the lack of clarity in parts of both texts, led Stuhlmueller to hold that we are on shaky foundations if we try to *prove* the authenticity of Jesus as Messiah from the psalms or other Old Testament texts. However, according to Stuhlmueller, once we have come to faith in Christ, the Old Testament prophecies and psalms come into clear and sharp focus. Faith in Christ is deeper than rational conviction, it is what is "revealed to Simon by my Father in Heaven"!

Psalm 110 is full of rather mystical phrases like "from the womb of the morning," the dawn being seen as deliverance from the feared underworld. "Like dew your youth will come"—the ancients did not know how dew was formed and it became a symbol of the mysterious and imperceptible workings of God. "The holy mountains," of course, are those of Jerusalem, above all Mount Zion. "You are a priest of the order of Melchisedech" adds a new dimension: he will be a Messiah-King-Priest. There was that mysterious meeting between the priest Melchisedech with Abraham, father of the Jewish faith, when the latter acknowledged the priestly role of this priest-king of Salem. The Davidic Messiah-Priest-King to come kneels to drink from the stream by the way. That is a humble act of one who knows all his kingly and priestly authority is from YHWH. For that act, which symbolizes his total acknowledgment of YHWH-Saviour, the priest-king is exalted to fulfill the work of the Messiah.

From the beginning of humankind's history, fractured continually by violence, betrayal, compromise, and war, every people has longed for a perfect leader to guide them out of their tragic mess. The Chinese created an emperor they called Son of Heaven, who was their priest as well as ruler. The religious rites he performed at the New Year, they believed, would bring a bountiful harvest and affect even the cosmic powers. The Japanese Emperor, descendent of the Sun Goddess and Supreme High Priest of Shinto, plants the first rice seedlings and harvests the first grain in autumn. These sacred acts, his subjects trust, will benefit the paddy fields the length and breadth of Japan. King Arthur of Camelot was a dream of the English people. The euphoria that greeted John F. Kennedy's first promises about "the New Frontier" showed the old yearning to be very much alive. But the hype of U.S. newspapers was essentially different from the "hyperbole" in the Royal Messianic Psalms. The latter were the Word of God, impossible yearnings at first sight, but fulfilled beyond the words in the Divine Son who became man.

Israel Zolli was a Jew born in 1881 in what is now Poland. His happy contacts since childhood with tolerant Catholic neighbors gave him an early interest in Jesus of Nazareth. After university and rabbinical studies in Florence he became chief Rabbi of Trieste in 1914. From 1930–38 he taught Hebrew in the University of Padua, publishing *The Nazarene* in 1938. In 1940 he became Chief Rabbi of Rome. When the Germans occupied Rome in 1943 he advised his fellow Jews to disbelieve secular assurances and go into hiding, which he himself did while remaining active in the Jewish cause. Through such activity he came into contact with Pius XII and grew to admire him greatly.

Zolli meanwhile continued his studies on the Nazarene and Catholicism. During the Yom Kippur services of 1944 he said he saw Jesus present with the congregation. That night he confided this to his wife, who replied that she also had seen Jesus during the services. They began formal studies with a Jesuit and on February 13, 1945, were received into the Catholic Church. Zolli described his long and sometimes painful journey in *Before the Dawn*, published in 1954. Speaking to academic friends in Rome he said conversion became a necessity when he concluded that only in the person of Jesus of Nazareth could he make full sense of the Old Testament prophecies about the Davidic Messiah and the Suffering Servant of Isaiah.

Israel Zolli died in 1956. I first heard of him from Rev. Dr Harry Davis the much loved dean of Bible Studies at the Catholic Institute of Sydney (formerly Manly Seminary). While Harry Davis was studying for his doctorate in philosophy in Rome during World War II, he became part of Mgr. O'Flaherty's network in the Vatican. You might have seen this Scarlet Pimpernel-like saga acted out by Gregory Peck in the movie *The Scarlet and the Black*. With the private approval of Pius XII, the Irish monsignor set up a highly successful organization that hid people being hunted by Nazis and Fascists, including Jews of course, and spirited them to safe places.

After gaining his PhD, Dr Davis began his Masters in Scripture at the Biblical Institute. It was now after the war and Zolli was teaching Semitics there, as well as at the University of Rome. Davis heard his story first-hand and his retelling of it to me some years later impressed me. In 1991 when I was doing research in Rome, I made some visits to the library at the Jewish-Christian institute run by Sisters of Our Lady of Zion. I read Zolli's *Before the Dawn* (New York, 1954) in which he describes his and his wife's conversion after they "saw the Nazarene during Yom Kippur services." The library also carried the spirited Jewish replies to Zolli's conversion, which I also read.

Religious conversion, like romance between people of different cultural backgrounds, can bring great sadness, anger and upheaval to others. Very understandably, practicing Jews regarded Zolli as a traitor (c/f L.I.Newman's "A 'Chief Rabbi' of Rome Becomes a Catholic: a Study in Fright and Spite" (New York, 1945)). I think very few of us who practice a religion are altogether at ease when a fellow believer "goes over" to another faith. There is an added reason for Jewish pain in this event which became poignantly obvious to me while I was studying in Jerusalem.

I spent six months in the Holy Land doing Biblical courses run by the Chicago Theological Union. One of my research projects was the detailed history of Christian persecution of Jews. I was shocked to read chapter and verse of almost two millennia of injustices, murders, rapes, torture, ghettos and pogroms—often "in the holy name of Jesus"! For long, sustained eras Christians seemed hellbent on nothing less than Jewish extinction. Given that history, I can well understand the Jewish pain, anger and sense of betrayal when a fellow religionist—above all a chief rabbi—asks for baptism.

There was one encouraging side of my grim perusal of the history of persecution of Jews: the depths of almost superhuman courage, and faith in The Name and the covenant that saved Judaism from extinction. With all of us, pain is as much a part of maturing into spirituality and compassion as winter storms are part of nature's fruitfulness. You see this in Jeremiah, Isaiah and the psalmists they inspired in the dark Babylonian winter. I could see it also in some magnificent Jewish personalities forged in the fires of medieval and modern persecution.

Yes, it is moving to study the beauty of the human spirit stretched to choose greatness over compromise and comfort. But that of course is no excuse for Christians not looking into the Jewish eyes of Jesus as he repeats that reproach, why are you persecuting me?

Faith is a mysterious thing because it is a gift from God. Psalm 36:9 puts it: "In you YHWH is the source of life. In your light we see light." The old Testament is full of references to the coming Messiah but we need God's light, God's gift of faith, to comprehend them. In Jesus' final instructions to the apostles before the Ascension, Luke 24: 44–47, he said: "'This is what I meant . . . that everything written about me, in the law [Torah] of Moses, in the prophets, and in the psalms must be fulfilled.' Then he opened their minds to understand the Scriptures . . ." The psalms are a field in which messianic gold is hidden, gold that is only discovered "by your light"—by seeking that light in prayer, "seeking the light of your face."

17 Hammarskjöld and Thérèse of Lisieux

D AG HAMMARSKJÖLD, SON OF THE PRIME MINISTER OF SWEDEN, made his own mark very quickly as a young academic teaching economics at Stockholm University. He was regarded as a prodigy, advanced quickly up the ladder of politics, and at age thirty-six became Chairman of the Bank of Sweden. In 1953, aged forty-eight, he became Secretary General of the United Nations. He stood his ground against Russian political thuggery but also against the lingering colonial thinking of some western nations. In 1961 he died in a plane that was probably booby-trapped. A month after his death he was awarded the Nobel Peace Prize. Among his well-concealed private papers was his diary, which made a remarkable impression worldwide when it was published as *Markings* in 1964.

The diary, begun when he was twenty years old, portrays the sufferings of a strangely complicated and often tortured man. Contemporaries would have been amazed to know this highly successful academic and politician was so unsure of himself. Pessimistic and cynical remarks abound about the "masks" he and other public figures wore, about his cowardice and hypocrisy. There are sometimes near total doubts about himself and whether life is worthwhile, and even "enticing thoughts" about suicide. He had long lost any of the Christian optimism he had imbibed as a boy.

Then comes the total change with his first diary entry for 1953:

> For all that has been—Thanks!
> To all that will be—Yes!

From that date on it is the diary of a different man. Suddenly his brilliant but often unhinged insights and breathtaking but blurred poetic intuitions have come into sharp focus. His writings change to those of a man confident in the faith. Scripture texts all at once blossom throughout the pages, like the wild flowers that suddenly appeared through the last snow and thrilled him as he tramped his beloved Swedish mountains in early spring. Not surprisingly the psalms appear more than another part of the Scriptures. He quotes them twenty-five times. The diary has become a love poem and he has discovered that the psalter can express, better than any other source book, the peace and thanksgiving now welling up from his new heart.

I was pleased to note that Hammarskjöld twice quotes Psalm 73, regarded by Stuhlmueller as one of the greatest. The psalm takes up a problem as old as our race, and the central problem in Job. Jeremiah 12:1 puts it bluntly: "You are always right when I dispute against you, Lord! Even so, I'd like to argue a matter of justice with you. Why is it that bad people make out so prosperously, that scoundrels end up living so contentedly?" That problem had once troubled Hammarskjöld as it troubles many today. It calls to mind that brilliant but chilling Japanese movie *The Worse the Rascal the Better He Sleeps*!

It's not just the contradiction of so many virtuous people doing ruggedly in life that worries the composer(s) of Psalm 73. He is an official of some kind in the temple—a levite, a liturgical singer, a sacristan? He is like believing Christian parents today whose children decide to vote with the majority: Sunday church is for the feeble-minded, Christian morality is old hat. Sleeping around, abortion if required, adultery, and euthanasia are democratic rights. The composer of Psalm 73 is troubled personally by the contradiction of so many scoundrels doing well in life and so many virtuous doing poorly. He is also troubled as one responsible for the faith of others, and many can identify with him.

Verse 1 begins with a statement of faith: God is good to us believing Israelites. Then verse 2 comes out with it: I almost gave up at seeing so many wicked get rich and arrogant. Verses 4–10 are a bitter denunciation of all the slick crooks who very successfully feather their own nests, not even hesitating to use violence when it furthers their interests. And so (v. 10–11) many believers begin to follow their lead, impressed by their success, and end up doubting if it makes any difference whether anyone tries to follow the Bible or not (v. 11-12).

Then a sudden outburst of personal bitterness, spoken straight at YHWH—"I have kept my heart clean and washed my hands in vain! You afflict me [with misery] day in and day out, you offer me [nothing but] chastisement, and dish it out from early dawn!" The washing of hands, as in Psalm 26:6, was a liturgical ceremony proclaiming freedom from guilt, something like our sacrament of reconciliation. The psalmist is very much a temple person and suddenly he fears his outburst is close to blasphemy. He is like the parent who—sick and tired of the strain and tension of believing and going to Mass despite its apparent uselessness—suddenly thinks of the children, and of what giving up on Jesus will mean to them, and has terrible feelings of guilt.

So verse 15 finds the psalmist calmer, quietly going over the problem again in his own mind, though this had become a real and distasteful effort. He goes into "your sanctuaries." This is the Hebrew plural of intensity, simply meaning the sanctuary, the temple. Reflecting in that quiet place, he has a deep realization of how fleeting is the wealth of evil-doers and how terrified they will be when death stalks them (v. 17–20). The psalmist is flooded with shame as he realizes how embittered he had become. Was "the piercing of his loins" some physical sickness he had? Loins can mean inmost soul. His condition might have been burnout, or even clinical depression. Whatever it was, it caused deep suffering.

Then in Verse 23, there is what Stuhlmueller calls a "leap of love and intuition." Despite his thoughts of giving up on YHWH, he had come here to the temple, seeking God's response, and YHWH "held him by his right hand," an expression of love. The next verse is a strong act of trust that YHWH will continue to guide him and even "receive him in glory." Does that mean eternal life with YHWH, heaven? Stuhlmueller and other commentators point out how in the early psalms there is no belief in heaven—colorless, consciousness Sheol is everyone's final destination. God, continues Stuhlmueller, used the belief of surrounding nations in conscious life after death to lead Israelites slowly to knowlege of and desire for heaven. It is certainly evident in the martyrology of the Maccabees, for instance, under the tyrant Antiochus Epiphanes (ruled 175–163 BC). The Sadducees of Jesus' day still held to the old tradition of a consciousless Sheol (Matt 22:23). A. A. Anderson sees in this "glory" a "tentative venture" to go beyond Sheol, "a glimpse rather than a firm faith." A close study of the psalms reveals "the development of doctrine" in the Bible. A serious but open-minded biblical student will come to see that the Word of God is no road map with streets, traffic lights, intersections and road numbers marked in! Only by "seeking him," often in obscurity or even darkness, do we discover YHWH's will for each one of us.

Notice how the psalmist gives no intellectual reasons why he withdraws his complaints against God's injustice, nor why he rejects his temptation to give up on YHWH and the temple liturgies. He just says he is overwhelmed by a sudden experience, alone in the temple, of God's presence, of his utter reliability and love:

> You held my hand . . . will receive me into glory . . . are my heart's rock, my own, God for all time . . . My delight here on earth is in nothing but You . . . My happiness comes from being close to God . . . My joy comes from being close to him and making the Lord my refuge. I shall publicly proclaim your wonderful deeds.

There it is, the believer who almost gave up, renewed while praying alone in the temple, given new energy to continue, confidently ready to bolster the faith of those who depend on him spiritually. It is Job all over again, battered, almost broken, Job who cried out bitterly: "A man becomes a laughing stock . . . if he cries to God and expects an answer!" (Job 12:4). Yet Job kept seeking God, and in him some meaning to the series of tragedies that wiped out his children, his livelihood, his health, and, almost, his sanity. His friends, the unhelpful "Job's comforters," taunt him for his simple trust in YHWH. But then the magnificent climax in chapter 42 that has made this account one of the world's great texts. Repenting of the way he has argued with YHWH, "holding forth on matters too deep for me, wonders beyond my ken . . . being an obstacle to your providence," Job exults: "I knew you before by words [people used] about you, but now my own eye has seen you!"

That's the personal, direct experience of God. St Thérèse of Lisieux was so fiercely tempted with doubts and plunged into darkness that, she revealed to her sister, suicide became a real temptation. Early in 1896 the 23 year-old Carmelite nun collapsed with tuberculosis and never recovered. She died eighteen months later. During her last illness she was racked with pain, and underwent a strong temptation against faith. Shortly before dying, she said: "I did not think it was possible to suffer so much." Her final words were: "My God, I love you." A few years before, her superior, a neurotic, mercurial, jealous-of-authority woman, told her to write the story of her life. Published after her death, *Story of a Soul* sold a million copies within the first fifteen years without any professional promotion. Fifty years later, in a France ravaged by World War II, it was the nation's best-seller after the Bible. Worldwide, readers reported miracles of grace and of physical healing after asking Thérèse's intercession. Pope Pius XI canonized her in 1925, calling this "a hurricane of glory." In her book Thérèse identifies herself with "this poor man," the *ani* of Psalm 34:7. *Ani* (plural *anawim*) appears in so many psalms after the humiliation of Babylon. An *ani* is someone who is convinced by experience of his or her poverty but equally convinced by experience that God is real and loving. This conviction is strong despite any number of indications to the contrary! Millions of twentieth century *anawim*, who were struggling with feelings of uselessness and even worthlessness because their lives seemed to have no impact on the problems surrounding them, gained new vision and energy from the "little" Carmelite's book. Thérèse said she loved reading the Bible itself rather than reading about the Bible. There are many biblical quotes in her autobiography and, significantly, quotes from the psalms far outnumber all others. Many readers of Thérèse have followed her example and begun reading the Bible daily.

Thérèse Martin (her family name) felt a great bond with Mary, which is hardly surprising in a Carmelite. She reacted against the tendency of some nineteenth-century Catholics to make Mary an empress far removed from ordinary life, as if Mary had been a woman who never knew the pain and darkness of a struggling wayfarer.

Thérèse would have been delighted with Paul VI's little masterpiece on Mary entitled *Marialis Cultus* (1974). In section 56 he wrote: "Mary in fact is one of our race, a true daughter of Eve—though free of that mother's sin—and truly our sister, who as a poor and humble woman fully shared our lot." But of course Mary's not just our sister. In the words of that touching hymn about Mary's visitation to Elizabeth, she is our "Little Sister Who Carried the Sun." Jesus had made her our mother and her prayers are of great power, as Thérèse and most of us have experienced. Above all, Thérèse discovered that she who told the waiters at Cana "do whatever he tells you," leads us also to obey her son, and to seek his face in the Scriptures.

18 *Little Sister Who Carried the Sun*

ST THÉRÈSE OF LISIEUX WAS A MEMBER OF THE ORDER OF Mount Carmel, a "Carmelite," and so formed in a very ancient tradition in which Mary is of tremendous importance. Mount Carmel was the place where the prophet Elijah stood up to one of the real nasties of the Bible, Queen Jezebel, who tried to lead the Israelites into the worship of Baal. Elijah challenged her to a spiritual contest. She assembled 450 priests of Baal on Mount Carmel, where they and Elijah killed sacrificial bulls. The challenge was to bring down fire from the heavens to consume the sacrifice. The followers of Baal went first and begged their god to show Israel that he was the true god by sending his famed lightning. Baal worshipers believed he personally sent the lightning that split open the skies for the vital late-autumn rains. The priests of Baal pranced and danced but nothing happened. Then Elijah prayed and YHWH sent fire that consumed his sacrificial bull. The victorious end of the story? Not a bit! Jezebel took out a contract on Elijah's life. The prophet went on the run until, exhausted in body and spirit, he begged the Lord to take his life. Instead, YHWH's angel gave him nourishment and told him to get up and return to the source, the roots of the covenant people, Mount Sinai. There Elijah was led to see that God is not discovered in roaring wind, storm, and lightning, let alone in gross political bullying like Jezebel's, but in "a gentle *ruah*." *Ruah* is the Hebrew word, fittingly feminine in gender, for breath, wind, or spirit. Christian tradition has interpreted Elijah's experience to mean the need to go out in the desert, such as Sinai, to be alone with the Father who speaks like a gentle wind or breath through his *ruah* YHWH, his Holy Spirit. In the Gospels, Jesus keeps going alone to remote deserts and mountains. God's *ruah*, which strengthened Elijah, prepared Jesus for his mortal combat.

In 1099, an international group of Christian soldiers took Jerusalem from Islam. Some of these Christian soldiers decided the best way to please God and protect Christian pilgrims to the Holy Land was not in the fighting of wars! They formed a prayer community that settled in caves on Mount Carmel and encouraged one another in seeking to hear the gentle *ruah*. Pilgrims from Europe joined them and by 1112 the Bishop of Jerusalem had written them a rule of life. The Carmelites had begun their magnificent history.

A special Catholic (and Orthodox) phenomenon soon entered the Carmelite story: they began to experience a special presence and influence of the Mother of Jesus. In place of the Crusader's tunics they came to don the brown scapular as the livery of her "knights." The Marian dimension of the knight, a powerful feature of later medieval chivalry, was manifesting itself spiritually. Two saints and spiritual writers of great influence who wore this brown Carmelite livery are Teresa of Avila and her helper John of the Cross, in the sixteenth century. Countless people down to our own day have associated themselves with the Carmelites by wearing the simplified brown scapular. St Thérèse of Lisieux, in the book she wrote only because she was told to, spoke to millions of moderns about the Carmelite ideal of contemplation, of "treasuring these things in the heart" like Mary, Christ's humble disciple who also became a dynamic presence for countless Christians.

Thérèse, with a childlike simplicity that was really a charism, tells us how she began the book that was to stir generations:

> Before taking up my pen, I knelt down before the statue of Mary—the one that has given so many proofs of the Queen of Heaven's maternal love for our [Carmelite] family. I asked her to guide my hand so that I might not write one line displeasing to her.

Why write all this about Mary, in a book on the psalms? I do it as a lead up to Mary's own psalm, the Magnificat (Lk 1:46–56). There are a number of songs or psalms sung by women in the Old Testament. Moses' elder sister Miriam, in Exodus 15:21, "took up a timbrel, and all the women followed her with timbrels, dancing. And Miriam led them in the refrain: 'Sing of YHWH: He has covered himself in glory, horse and rider he has thrown into the sea.'" Apparently the ancient Israelites sang or recited psalms much as we do today. Miriam's refrain was what we call "the response" and was repeated like a chorus all through Moses' psalm ("The Song of Victory," Ex. 15:1–18). Deborah, the first of Israel's valiant women, inspired a great victory over Jabin's Canaanites and their 900 chariots plated with iron. With army commander Barak, she sang a war cry psalm called "The Song of Deborah" (Judg 5). Judith, the beautiful young widow who is said to have beguiled and then beheaded the Assyrian general whose troops were about to take Jerusalem, leads the people in a psalm about her own daring in Judith 16:1–21.

There is another great woman psalmist in the Old Testament, Hannah, "whom YHWH had made barren." She too was a valiant woman, not warlike like Deborah and Judith, but of heroic trust in the Lord. Refusing to give up even when it seem hopeless, the taunted Hannah went on pilgrimage to the temple of YHWH in Shiloh

(Jerusalem did not yet exist). Her prayer was heard and she bore a son who became one of the great prophets, Samuel. In 1 Samuel 2:1–10 she sings her psalm, "The Song of Hannah." A kind of forerunner to Mary's Magnificat psalm, it also is Messianic. At a time when Israel had no king she sings in 2:10: "YHWH endows his king with power and exalts the strength of his anointed." Like the Magnificat it is a song of the poor, the *anawim* that appear with increasing frequency after Zephaniah 2:3. However, Hannah's song lacks the extraordinary simplicity, personalism, and warmth of the Magnificat and its blend of gentleness and strength. One Japanese commentator calls the Magnificat "the Song of Mary, Bamboo of God." Bamboo is gentle, its fronds responding to the slightest wind. It is also strong and reliable. The autumn cyclones that leave a trail of uprooted forest giants cannot tear the bamboo from its hold on the ground. "Humility" comes from the Latin word *humus*, meaning earth, ground, soil. The humble are solidly grounded, like the bamboo, while the hubris of uprooted mountain giants proved to be groundless.

Mary's Magnificat, Luke 1:47–53, has been put to music by countless composers and its scenario painted by numberless artists. The Protestant Bible scholar William Barclay quotes with approval Stanley Jones' accolade: "The Magnificat is the most revolutionary statement in the world." Exaggerated? The New Zealand monthly, *Marist Messenger*, August 1992, ran an article, "A Reflection on Nossa Senhora of Brazil," by Barry Malone SM. During the Argentine military dictatorship and heavy censorship, the government attempted to suppress Luke 1:52–53: "He has deposed the mighty from their posts and raised the lowly to high positions. He has enriched the hungry with good things and sent the wealthy off empty." Certainly the Romans who governed Israel as their own possession would also have regarded these words and those of verse 51, "He has routed the arrogant," as aimed at them and treasonous. The slip of a lass from Nazareth proved stronger than Roman and Argentinian generals. Mary qualifies as the greatest of Israel's valiant women.

Some get disturbed by the questions: Are these the words of Mary? How can we be sure? Vatican II's Constitution on Revelation, Chapter 3, presents an all-important principle for Catholics, already quoted but worth repeating here and more fully:

> Therefore, since everything asserted by the inspired authors or sacred writers must be held to be asserted by the Holy Spirit, it follows that the books of Scripture must be acknowledged as teaching firmly, faithfully and without error that truth which God wanted put into the sacred writings *for the sake of our salvation.*

The Magnificat is the Holy Spirit telling us what kind of person Mary was, maybe having her say more than she would have said of herself because of her humility! How often at a celebration like a fiftieth wedding anniversary the wife and husband falter in speaking about themselves while their sons and daughters recount their virtues with glowing words. Be that as it may, in the final analysis, Mary's Magnificat is Mary described by the Holy Spirit.

This Mary is a person who loves the Scriptures. She responds to Elizabeth's lyric greeting with an insightful medley of Old Testament tunes. Her first two lines are found in 1 Samuel 2:1, Isaiah 61:10, and Habakkuk 3:18. You get a lot more from Scripture when you study its contexts. Habakkuk 3:18 is at the end of one of the outstanding passages of the Old Testament. The prophet is writing around the time of Jeremiah when Israel was on the rack and the Jews were muttering about God not keeping his promise to protect his people. Habakkuk responds with a magnificent statement of total trust in verse 17, the one preceding the Magnificat's quote about "exulting in God my savior." Verse 16 runs: "Even if the fig trees do not flower nor the vines produce any grapes, though the olive crop fails and the fields are infertile, sheep vanishing from the folds and cattle from the sheds . . . I will exult in God my savior." Mary's Israel was similar to Habakkuk's. Judah and her kings were weak, humiliated, subservient to mighty foreign forces. Habakkuk sees the human misery, but looks beyond to God and rejoices.

Mary describes herself in terms of the lowly *anawim* of the psalms, protesting she is a *doulos* ("slave" in Luke's Greek). Slaves occupied the lowest rank in society. But because of God's graciousness, "all future generations will call me blessed." What a contrast in one person—a lowly slave yet possessed of a magnanimity that is global! Called blessed until the end of time! As stated earlier, the greatest Japanese haiku contrast the transience and weakness of creatures with the abiding reliability of the All Merciful One. The Magnificat is a kind of extended haiku. "His mercy [*eleos*, which is the Greek for *hesed*] reaches to every generation of God-fearing people" (a quote from Ps 103:17). "Holy is his name" is Psalm 111:96. YHWH's treatment of the lowly, the *anawim*, *vis-à-vis* the proud is proclaimed by Mary with quotations from Psalm 138:6, Sirach (also called Ecclesiasticus) 33:12, and Job 5:11. Ezechiel 17:24 presents the same message. Psalm 89:10 has YHWH scattering his enemies, the evil who are given the cosmic name Rahab, the serpent of the Waters of Chaos. "The hungry he has given good things" is from Psalm 107:9 and his "help to Israel his servant, mindful of his mercy [*hesed*]" from Psalm 98:3. "His servant Israel" is Isaiah 41:9. The promise to Abraham and his descendants is made in Genesis 12:3, 13:15, and 22:18—and is one of the fundamental revelations of the Old Testament. The New Testament has thirty-two references to Abraham our spiritual father, nine of them in Paul. Luke's Magnificat verse 50, "His mercy is from age to age," employs *eleos* for mercy. This is the Greek word used to translate the Old Testament word *hesed*, which runs through the psalms like the vital pointer stars that kept old-time mariners on their true course.

Mary's Magnificat is classically psalmistic by its appeal to God's acts in Israel's salvation history. Mary refers to YHWH's revelation and oath to Abraham, she quotes texts that center on his *hesed* fidelity. The Magnificat rejoices in his helping the oppressed, such as Hannah who became mother of the spiritual hero Samuel, and his protection of his "servant" Israel, a favorite expression in Isaiah. In all this she is one with the psalmists in the message of salvation history: This is what faithful YHWH has done, and this is also what he is doing NOW. The "marvels" or "great things" done for Mary by YHWH in verse 49 is the very same word used by Moses in Deuteronomy 10:21 for the great things done by YHWH in Egypt to break Pharaoh's iron grip on YHWH's people.

The spiritual athletes of the first centuries of Christianity, called the Fathers (Justin, Irenaeus, Polycarp, Origen, the three Gregorys, Chrysostom, Ambrose, Augustine, etc.), were able to found the Christian churches in the teeth of persecution, wild heresies, and strong political opposition because of their utter belief that the Scriptures were inspired by the Holy Spirit—they were not like the Greek and Roman classics, haphazard human documents. The Fathers continuously studied and above all prayed the Scriptures, discovering in them a conviction and joy so great that their preaching convinced great minds and simple townsfolk despite the huge sociological obstacles. Vatican II recalls Catholics to personal reading and praying of the Scriptures. We Catholics owe much to the Protestants in this modern return to the Bible. They understood better the need to read the Scriptures at home as well as hear homilies at church that centered on them.

Protestant Scripture scholars pioneered modern biblical studies and were well to the fore until recent years. Catholics learned a great deal by listening to them. But it has now become a two-way dialogue. Many Protestants are taking a new look at Mary and her role in the Christian life. Methodist clergyman Joseph Neville Ward became deeply involved in the British ecumenical movement. He decided to try praying the rosary to understand Catholics better. To his surprise he found it thoroughly scriptural and wrote a book about the rosary, *Five for Sorrow, Ten for Joy*, that has been widely read in both Catholic and Protestant circles. Probably the outstanding Anglican theologian of the last two decades, John Macquarrie, wrote the book *Mary for All Christians* just a few years ago. It was well received in Protestant circles.

A serious study of history shows the abiding human tendency of going to one extreme or the other. It's hard to get a balance. Many Catholics of Luther's day went to extremes with devotion to Mary. Luther reacted vigorously against these "terrible papist proportions." But Luther did not reject devotion to Mary as the sinister danger later perceived by Protestants. In his last sermon, January 17, 1546, when death was in the offing, Luther said: "Is Christ alone to be adored? Or is the holy Mother of God rather not to be honored? This is the woman who crushed the serpent's head. Hear us [Mary]. For your Son denies you nothing."

If we Catholics imitate Mary as the Holy Spirit portrays her in the Magnificat—a woman imbued with the Scriptures—we will surely be able to present her, and Catholicism, in a truer light to our Protestant sisters and brothers. And listening humbly to the Scriptures, as she did, will help us listen more humbly to Protestants—recognizing God's salvation history deeds among them, and enriching ourselves with some of their wisdom. Surely both sides will benefit.

Jean Guitton, attempting to portray the extraordinary combination of simplicity and depth in the Magnificat, quotes a remark by the landscape painter Corot (1796–1875). Questioned about a canvas he had just completed Corot replied: "How much time did I spend on it? Five minutes—and my whole life." Guitton concludes: "The Magnificat might have lasted only the taking of five breaths; it tells the tale of a lifetime."

19 A Forty-Day Fast for a Blackbird Song

Psalm 104

THERE HAD BEEN A LITTLE MIST THAT COOL MORNING IN EARLY May and the sun's rays suddenly slanted through and touched the tiptop of a young pin oak. I gasped: the leaves had turned to a golden red, shining brilliantly against the summer-green on the rest of the tree! Then I realized that it was nothing extraordinary. The pin-oak leaves change to autumn reds and browns and yellows from the very top first, and then gradually down the tree. But for a moment it had seemed the sun's rays had touched the leaves and instantaneously colored them. Mount Fuji is not far west of the date line. Japanese love to climb the majestic mountain during the night and share in its dawn moments of glory—it is the first part of earth touched by the rays of the new day. Whether those in the Siberian mountains dispute that claim I am not sure, but I know that dawn on Mount Fuji is an experience of awe and wonder.

G. K. Chesterton's legs might not have carried the great man to the top of Fuji-san but, had they, I am sure his eyes and heart would have rejoiced with the Japanese climber-pilgrims. The vision of Chesterton's poetry helped his generation, and his many enthusiastic readers three generations after his death, to retain the vital sense of wonder. He was the poet of awe *par excellence*, alerting us to startling beauty everywhere. He wrote, in *Orthodoxy*: "[I felt] men might fast forty days for the sake of hearing a blackbird song . . . might go through fire to find a cowslip." The cowslip is a very insignificant English wild-flower found in marshes and swamps. Greenies will chain themselves to bulldozers to save a threatened species. Good, but Chesterton's wonder and awe went deeper than the threatened flora and fauna. His eye and heart went to the more amazing Source of it all.

Cicero once wrote about the Latin word *religio* (religion in English), giving various opinions put forward concerning its origin. One suggestion was that it came from *re legere*, to read again, to look at again. A religious mind keeps taking second looks at apparently mundane things and events, and discovering transcendental meanings there. By this definition alone you would have to say the psalmists were great religionists. Their poetry is continually overwhelmed by the sheer beauty and grace they discovered all around them. Their sense of awe and wonder at nature, especially seen in the clear light of revelation that all beauty and fruitfulness comes from the creator's *hesed* (steadfast love), overflowed into the Psalms of Praise. These are a very significant part of the psalter. Psalm 104 is a magnificent example. Its grandeur, its blend of power and gentleness expresses in poetry what Beethoven nobly attempted to say with his Piano Concerto in D Major. The psalm begins with the deeds of the Cosmic Artificer, stretching out the firmament as the earth's protective tent, controlling the Waters of Chaos, riding on the wings of the wind, creating and controlling fire to be his servant. Having fixed mother earth on unshakeable foundations he drew the seas around her as outer garments. The Waters of Chaos, terrible and unpredictable foes to Israel's nature-worshiping neighbors, become humble mountain springs at the service of small birds and wild donkeys! (vv. 10–11). These waters are made gentle under YHWH's hand, so that they nourish pasturelands for farm animals and make fertile the tilled fields that provide his people with "the bread of the strong and wine to make them cheerful" (vv. 13–15).

This world that has come from the sure hands of the Creator is good and orderly. Even fearsome lions have their rightful place. At night they hunt for the prey God intended for them but with the daylight they disappear into their dens so that farmers may work their land without fear (vv. 21–23). The oceans that make distant trade and travel possible teem with life (v. 25). Under YHWH even Leviathen, the thing that terrified the Jews' neighbors, has found a positive role (v. 26). Every living creature has its place and purpose, the wild as well as the domesticated. Every element of nature, the terrifying as well as the lovely, is an integral part of a harmonious whole animated by *ruah* YHWH, the breath of his Spirit.

None of the beasts nor the elements rebel against the Creator's wise providence. Only creatures with the most breathtaking gift of all—free will, which brings them closest to God—can mar the harmony. Some will regard submission as slavery and cry out: I will not serve! Others will demand sameness for all, and accuse the Creator of unjust favoritism for giving special gifts to some or of cruelty because carnivorous creatures eat flesh and fish. Others will petulantly claim the right to live as they please and reject the old wisdom: "God always forgives, man sometimes forgives, nature never forgives." Dying of self-inflicted ills, they will curse God for their misfortunes.

The composer of Psalm 104 has seen this and his one negative judgment rises to his lips: "May sinners vanish from the earth, may the evil cease to be" (v. 35). He however will praise YHWH for everything, "singing and playing for my God while I live. May these aspirations of mine give YHWH something of the pleasure he gives me . . . Bless YHWH my soul" (v. 33–34). As C. S. Lewis discovered several millennia later, searching for God, contemplating his gifts that abound in nature and in human life (farming, drinking wine, etc.) and blessing him and praising him for it all, expands the soul. The "singing and playing" of the psalms with others in temple liturgies filled the psalmist with pleasure. This joy in worship is a foretaste of the Beatific Vision in Heaven. Our minds and hearts will never tire of contemplating the Trinity, inexhaustible source of all the beauty and happiness we have ever experienced, and of the vast joys we have not yet had the capacity to experience. "Doc" Woodbury was magnificent when he described this Beatific Vision:

> containing not only the Ninth Symphony but the incomparably greater music Beethoven was too limited to compose . . . containing the joy of parents watching their beautiful child and inconceivably more; . . . the joy of a farmer surveying his field of corn, of a scientist writing up his new discovery.

C. S. Lewis found the Praise Psalms somewhat cloy for some time after his conversion. The word cloy originally meant "to lame a horse with a nail." Lewis hadn't known how lame he was as an agnostic who could only see beauty that was causeless, and therefore bordering on meaningless. The psalms led him to an experience, similar to a person separated as a child from his loving parents by war and after the rather grim life of a self-reliant and self-centered orphan finding he has a magnificent father, family, and home. Though shy and embarrassed at first, the "orphan" comes to believe and return the new experience of being loved unconditionally by a parent and siblings.

The first Buddha, the Indian Siddartha Gautama, was born into a wealthy aristocratic family about 563 BC. Early in his childhood, his mother, Princess Maya, died. Prince Siddartha's loss seems to have disposed him to a restlessness about the meaning of life. He received a liberal education, was trained to be proficient in the martial arts and become a fine horseman. He married, was blessed with a child, seemed to lack nothing, and yet was not at ease within himself. Life was beautiful, yes, but three cold shadows fell across human society and disturbed him deeply—sickness, aging, and death. They contradicted the goodness of existence. Unable to bear his growing angst and to forget the serenity of a beggar monk he once met, he slipped unseen out of his estates and became a penniless monk, living by a begging bowl. He went visiting the ascetics in the forests, tried to pray like them and almost killed himself with austerities. Sadly he concluded he could not force open the mysterious gates to enlightenment by sheer asceticism. How then? He had tried so hard. Would he never discover peace and truth?

He did not give up. Some short time later he was up before the dawn, as was his habit, seated in the lotus position beneath a linden tree. He gazed transfixed at the morning star and suddenly exclaimed: "That is me shining!" The great gulf between him and other creatures that had given him a sense of opposition and alienation had been bridged. He had been granted an intuition into Transcendental Being, and he was part of that wonderful Reality. A great peace flooded Siddartha, and an unknown joy. From it flowed compassion for other discouraged seekers and indeed for all living creatures. For the rest of his life he would labor unswervingly and fruitfully to bring his experience to others. The light of the morning star was not, surely, the only light that had flooded his being! He had been enlightened from within by the Father of all compassion.

We rely on spoken legends for Siddartha's story. Maybe there is some exaggeration, but the core experience is so true that it changed the face and heart of Asia. One of the great new virtues the Buddha experienced and taught was awareness, awareness of the life around us. A true Buddhist will sometimes bow in gratitude before eating a bowl of rice because bountiful nature and the labor of so many good people have produced it. A farming family dug and flooded the paddy field, then planted and harvested the rice. Laborers carried it to the storehouse and husked it. Some dug the clay for the rice bowls, an artisan shaped it and placed it in a kiln fired by his helpers. If we are aware, we are filled with gratitude and praise.

People who strive to be aware of all the seeking and praying and loving that has made the psalms, begin to feel their heartbeat, which is the *hesed* and *rahamin* love of YHWH for all his creatures, from monster whales of the deep to wild donkeys and tiny fledglings in forests—but above all for the ones he made in his own likeness.

As said earlier, Psalm 104 has expressions and concepts found in the earlier Egyptian hymn to Aten, or Aton as it sometimes written, composed by the monotheist Pharaoh Akenaten (c. 1364–1374 BC). Scholars like Stuhlmueller and R. J. Williams like to point this out. There are many other psalms that have borrowed from "pagan" hymns. This should surely lead Scripture-centered people to an awareness of the Holy Spirit also at work among non-biblical people. Among today's very important Christian books are those of the monk Bede Griffiths. Converted to the faith as a student at Oxford he joined the Benedictines, was eventually elected Prior of Farnborough Abbey, and in 1955 went to India to help pioneer a monastery there. He was a man of prayer, simple living, and asceticism. Water finds its own level. He began to meet non-Christian Indian holymen—some still living, others in India's ancient spiritual classics. He discovered in very many of them St Paul's "fruits of the Holy Spirit" (Gal 5:22): love, peace, magnamimity, joy, self-control, etc. Dom Griffiths rejoiced to see at work among these people of great goodwill the Kingdom of God. He rejoiced that the documents of Vatican II greatly influenced by the testimony of bishops and missionaries working among non-Christians, accepted wholeheartedly the working of Christ's grace among sincere believers of faiths other than ours.

One of the most influential theologians at Vatican II, Karl Rahner, wrote an article only a few years before his death that has been called his spiritual last will and testament. (You can find it in the Fall 1980 issue of *Theology Digest*, pages 221-5.) Rahner wrote that in the First Age of Christianity, Jewish spirituality and the Jerusalem temple were very central for Christians. Then in AD 70, the Romans destroyed Jerusalem and the temple. Surviving Jewish authorities, fearing Judaism could die out, refused to accept Christians as members of their religion. The Christians, many of whom had been born Jews, now centered their lives on Rome and the Greco-Roman world. This was the Second Age, when Christianity accepted what was good and true in Greek philosophy. St Justin, martyred at Rome in 165 is an early and seminal example of this. The Third Age, which Rahner calls soteriologically (salvation-wise) optimistic, began with Vatican II's call to Catholics to be open to and enriched by those things that are true and beautiful (and therefore from the Holy Spirit), not only in Judaism, Orthodoxy and Protestantism, but in the great religions such as Hinduism, Buddhism, and Islam.

One of the greatest deeds of Pope John Paul II, as far as Japanese Buddhists are concerned, was to invite them and other non-Christian leaders to Assisi to pray together for peace. They used no single bland prayer, with words so vague they would not offend anyone. No, each religion was invited to pray in its own words. The Pope, to the amazement of many, accepted and welcomed the validity and holiness of sincere prayers offered by non-Christians. This, I believe, is one of the things "the Spirit is saying to the Churches" at the end of the second millennium. I think the Spirit said this also when he brought some great non-Jewish religious hymns into the psalter.

20 Death, Last Steps on the Way Home

In the place where she was homeless
All men are at home.
(G. K. Chesterton, *The House of Christmas*)

"F OR AMONG THE DEAD NO ONE REMEMBERS YOU: IN THE nether world, who gives you thanks?" These words of Psalm 6:5 and similar ones in numerous other psalms reflect the Old Testament's quite negative teaching on the after life—up to the times of the heroic Maccabees, around 165 BC. Until that late stage the Bible did not teach heaven, that sharing in God's fullness of life and happiness enjoyed by the just after death. The Sadducees who confronted Jesus and Paul held doggedly to the literal and oft repeated teaching of the Scriptures up until Maccabean times—after death the soul enters the twilight world of Sheol, an all but consciousless state. The Sadducees urge this teaching in Luke 20:27 and Acts 23:8, for instance. They rigidly rejected the "development of doctrine" found in Jesus' reply: "You understand neither the Scriptures nor the power of God."

For most of the Old Testament, Jews did not have that immense hope founded on what Maccabean Jews and Christians call heaven. The ancient Jews obeyed YHWH (and recited the psalms) solely because of the peace and consciousness of his loving presence that accompanied this. They traveled those dangerous roads to Jerusalem reciting the Pilgrim Psalms for the same reason. As the times grew no better, the Jews found more and more consolation in the prophetic Messianic Psalms. These promised God's ultimate vindication of Israel, a future and glorious reign of justice and peace that he would establish. Jerusalem would become the all-powerful center of the whole world! Gradually the vision deepened and spirtualized until it became a hope above and beyond this material world, a happiness that "eye has not seen nor ear heard." The pilgrim journeys to beleaguered Jerusalem gradually took on the symbolic and transcendental dimension of a final journey to the New Jerusalem, the eternal Beatific Vision of God.

I've been amazed to discover how many Catholic priests lost a parent, especially a mother, in childhood. The hope of meeting again in heaven made bearable and meaningful the otherwise desperate loneliness of a motherless child. The loss forced the grieving child to look for peace and meaning beyond time and space. The modern English psychiatrist and writer Anthony Storr has remarked on the overwhelming number of famous poets and writers who lost their mother before they were five years old! The loss turned them into seekers.

The Japanese dictionary has many more words than its English equivalent. Especially numerous are emotionally and poetically evocative words. For instance, there are over twenty Japanese words for "rain," depending on whether it is early spring rain, summer thunderstorm rain, deep winter rain, etc. The two ideographs for the word AISHU—sadness, sorrow, grief—are a case in point. The first part, AI is made up of the ideographs for garment and mouth. In classical plays, such as kabuki, an actor brings the copious sleeve of his kimono up to his mouth to indicate crying, sadness. The second part, SHU, is made up of the ideographs for heart and autumn. The heart is sad in autumn, because the disappearing summer grasses and falling leaves remind Japanese, even more poignantly than the falling cherry blossoms in spring, of the essential transitoriness, evanescence, and impermanence of the material world, including human life. Yet autumn is precisely the time when many of the finest and deepest haiku poems are written. Basho's, for instance.

Classical Latin had the expression *tristitia rerum*, meaning the sadness at the heart of all (material) things. This emotive expression described the Romans' equivalent of the Japanese feeling in autumn, I believe. Morris West writes of the old Latin saying expressing the sadness that sweeps over many after sexual intercourse. It comes from the realization that the unity of even the most loving husband and wife never achieves totality and fullness. Once again, this strange "loneliness" can turn people into seekers after the complete unity and integration that only the Beatific Vision can give.

There is a magnificent haiku poem by Issa Kobayashi (1763–1827). He was born into a poor farming family in Nagano Prefecture, a then miserable mountainous area north-west of what is now Tokyo. Winters were harsh and the biting north wind often drove snow through crevices and cracks in young Issa's rough rural home. The lad would sometimes wake shivering to find snow on his bedclothes. Issa lost his mother when he was only four and her place was taken by a harsh stepmother. Life became so unbearable that the youth, aged fifteen and penniless, fled home for a very uncertain future in the capital, Edo. His life was dogged by tragedy, above all by the early deaths of his beloved wife and children. Yet as he lay dying he wrote a joyful farewell poem. Though almost 170 years have elapsed, the poem still glows like a blazing hearth on a raw winter's night: *ARIGATA YA FUSUMA NO YUKI MO JŌDO YORI*.

Translating Japanese haiku into another language is something like turning classical Gregorian chant into a modern English guitar tune! With misgivings I translate Issa's poem: "Ah, gratitude! The snow on my blanket, too, was from the Pure Land." The Pure Land, *Jōdo*, is the

Buddhist word for what Christians call heaven. Believers can enter the Pure Land if they put their trust in Amida's Mercy, and strive to live virtuously. Issa had come to see that his troubles and sufferings were not the measure of the universe. The universe and each journey, however difficult, were of inestimable worth and meaning because the heart of reality beat with the compassion of Amida, who lovingly leads believers to eternal life. Issa's words are surely "seeds of the Logos."

Many moderns no longer believe in heaven. For them the universe has become a vast wasteland without signposts. The neo-nonbelievers are in the main pessimistic. On the other extreme we have neo-Christians who are over-optimistic. I say neo-Christians because they no longer hold to one of the old truths Jesus kept emphasizing—God's judgment after death and the possibility of being lost forever! True, this is a great mystery. How could an all-loving God allow anyone to lose himself or herself forever! But then, to use the atheists' argument, if there exists an all-loving God how could that God allow little children to die of AIDS or even allow kittens to die of hunger and cold? This, like so much in our lives, is mystery we have to live with rather than understand. If we say we are believing Christians we don't throw out the parts of Jesus' teaching that are mysteries. (Unless, maybe, we are like that very confident preacher who said: "Now what Jesus was really trying to say was this"!)

Of course it doesn't help to try to "imagine" duration, in the soul's life after death. "Time" will surely be of a different dimension from the clock time we know here below.

Paul put it succinctly and bluntly in 2 Timothy 2:12–13. "If we disown him then he will disown us. We might be unfaithful but he is always faithful, for he cannot disown his own self." Paul repeatedly taught what Jesus taught: damnation is a very real possibility for all of us. Unthinkable? Many found his teaching on the Eucharist was unthinkable. Peter could not understand it but he accepted the mystery because Jesus taught it. That is the essence of biblical faith. That is "becoming like a child," which Jesus says is the condition for entering heaven. "My Father in heaven" reveals mysteries to "mere children."

A great light in my (frequently dim) schooldays was Fr Paddy McCarthy. He won the allegiance of us rugby-loving boys almost without opening his mouth—he had played half-back for that mighty team, the New Zealand All Blacks. As he bent low at the penitential rite at Mass we imagined him putting the ball into the scrum! Paddy taught us to love English literature, and to love the faith—and for him the faith was something very joyful. He died in 1976, aged eighty-three. I saw him not long before he died. The fleet-footed All Black was now feeble—Parkinson's Disease, I think. He had to shuffle his feet to start walking and his flesh sagged. When I asked how he was, Fr Mac's eyes sparkled and genuine humor spread over his face—making it quite beautiful. "Never better, Paul, never better," he replied. He was ready and happy to be going Home.

I still remember many of his stories that I heard as a schoolboy, stories that enlivened and focused his classes. One was about Cardinal Manning, the English convert. Though he wrote voluminously on spirituality, the cardinal had an embarrassing fear of dying. He confided this to a priest friend who, hearing that he was dying early in 1892, visited him. "How do you feel?" he asked the prelate with some apprehension. "Like a schoolboy the night before going home for the long holidays," was the reply, recalling that seventy years earlier the schoolboy Manning had suffered great homesickness when he entered Harrow as a boarder.

Joe Riley was the powerful, six-foot-plus blacksmith at a small settlement outside Casino, New South Wales, in Australia's pioneering days before the turn of this century.

An excellent horseman and without a trace of flabbiness, he was chosen as one of the small group of lancers sent to represent Australia at Queen Victoria's Diamond Jubilee, 1897. He married happily and was blessed with six children. Then disaster struck, leaving him a widower. His robust faith deepened and with all his children grown up he took vows as a coadjutor brother in the Society of Mary as Br Peter Chanel. I knew him when I was a boarder at Woodlawn College. The whole school loved and venerated him.

In September 1955 he was gravely ill in St Vincent's Hospital, Lismore, New South Wales. Fr Peter Guiren, on the Woodlawn staff, went to see him on September 17. As he entered the ward a solemn doctor beckoned him aside and told him Br Peter would not make it through the night. (Peter Guiren was later to become Marist Provincial and bemuse European counterparts and translators at General Assemblies in Rome with his penchant for metaphors from sporting arenas.) Fr Guiren was taken aback to hear that his old friend was dying, and thinking Br Peter had a right to know said: "I've just been talking with the umpire. He said the light is fading and you might have to close your innings tonight. Is there anything that you are worried about?" He felt a great surge of love and pity as he gazed on the sunken eyes and listened to the wheezing, labored breathing.

"I'm not exactly worried but . . . ," gasped the shrunken giant. "But?"—Guiren leaned closer. Was the marriage of a son or daughter in deep trouble, or did Br Peter need to unburden himself about some personal scruple before he met his Lord? "I'm not exactly worried but . . . it's just that I've never died before!" Then the beautiful, familiar smile lit up his tired features and told Peter Guiren that he was ready to go. He died that night.

A journey is a good one if it ends well. Psalm after psalm begins with a complaint, or fear, or even terror, only to end in praise. Talking and singing to God brought steadiness and then peace and joy to the psalmist. The joy became greater when YHWH's revelation gradually told believers that this happiness was but the prelude to "the torrent of joy" that is the participation in his eternal happiness. We cannot imagine heaven because, in the words of St Paul, "eye has not seen nor ear heard" the like. If by some miracle of mental growth a child in the womb could communicate with its mother, it could only believe, but not imagine the mother's glowing description of colors, birds' songs, the joy of its parents and siblings awaiting its birth in a spacious, happy home. This would be marvelously beyond comparison with the comfortable and safe but utterly confined and unfree womb! That is precisely the difference between our lives here on earth and the lives of the saints in heaven, the immeasurable home of Father, Son, and Holy Spirit.

Bibliography

Anderson, Bernhard W., *Out of the Depths* (Philadelphia: Westminister Press, 1974)

Anderson, A.A., *The Book of Psalms*, New Century Bible Commentary, 2 volumes (Grand Rapids: Eerdmans, 1981)

Carrel, Alexis, *Journey to Lourdes* (London: Hamish Hamilton, 1950)

Chesterton, G. K., *The Ballad of the White Horse* (London: Methuen, 1911)

—*Orthodoxy* (London: Bodley Head, 1908)

Craghan, John F., *The Psalms* (Wilmington: Michael Glazier, 1985)

Cranston, Ruth, *The Mystery of Lourdes* (London: Evans Brothers, 1956)

Gelin P.S.S., Albert, *The Poor of Yahweh* (Collegeville: Liturgical Press, 1963)

George S.M., Augustin, *Praying the Psalms* (Notre Dame, Indiana: Fides, 1964)

Hays, Edward, *St George and the Dragon* (Leavenworth: Forest of Peace Publishing, 1986)

Lewis, C. S., *Reflections on the Psalms* (London: Geoffrey Bles, 1958)

Petersen, Eugene H., *Where Your Treasure Is* (Grand Rapids: Eerdmans, 1985)

Stuhlmueller, C. P., Carroll, *Psalms 1*, Old Testament

Message, Volume 21 (Wilmington: Michael Glazier, 1983)

—*Psalms 2*, Old Testament Message, Volume 22 (Wilmington: Michael Glazier, 1983)

Tournay, Raymond, *Seeing and Hearing God with the Psalms* (Sheffield: Sheffield Academic Press, 1991)

Index

Index of Psalms